I am grateful for my dear friend Artur Simonyan. He is an amazing, godly leader in the body of Christ who walks in integrity and humility with wisdom. Artur lived in Kansas City for a season and prayed many hours a day in our prayer room at IHOPKC. In 2015, I visited his church in Armenia with my leadership team and saw with my own eyes how much God is using this man of God and his amazing team of leaders. Today, the Word of Life Church is the largest local church in Armenia, and it has one of the largest networks of churches in the Russian-speaking world. I recommend Artur's book because I believe it will strengthen and inspire many with its stories about Christian families and the feats of women during times of persecution in the Soviet Union. His book describes stories of families that raised children who are now strong leaders of the modern churches in the former Soviet countries. Several of those leaders live and serve the Lord in the United States today. This book contains an important warning, yet offers real hope and inspiration for all of us living in the end times.

— Mike Bickle
Best-Selling Author, Director, International House of Prayer

I met Bishop Arthur Simonyan A few years ago in Armenia, and my heart was impacted during the first hour we spent together. As Bishop Arthur shared his life with me, I realized I was sitting with someone who would shape the nations. Sometimes we think shaping a nation happens when we take the platform or public stage; yes, that's one way Bishop is shaping the nations. However, he is also bringing transformation one life at a time.

I watched him that day. A young man had come in from out of town and saw us while we were having lunch. Bishop stood up and engaged this young man in a deep conversation in just a few minutes. I could tell that this young man became his primary focus.

He encouraged him and made him feel as if his life mattered. It did, and it does!

As I think back on my own life, I can tell you I have been marked by the strength of my family, parents, and grandparents. I always remember the sacrifices they made for me, the times when I ran to my grandmothers' house in desperate need of prayer, and the unconditional love and acceptance that my mother and father lavished on me. This is a beautiful legacy that I will carry. Now, I love to tell my own children the stories of my childhood. It's as if I am creating a masterpiece with my words. Someday they will share these stories with their children and grandchildren.

Proverbs 13:22 tell us that a "good man leaves an inheritance to his children's children."

More important than material things we can leave to our children and grandchildren is the legacy of our lives. Our stories. Our testimonies. Our victories and defeats. These stories will build faith and strength to last generation after generation.

As you read *Sisters*, you will be touched by the real-life experiences of these modern-day heroes. You will be challenged and inspired to lead with strength and boldness. I want to encourage you to read through these stories, reflect, and ask yourself, *how can I use this testimony to make an impact in the lives of those around me?*

These women faced many oppositions. Every day they used their words and actions to shape their children and the lives around them. They cared, comforted, nurtured, loved, and laid down their lives for future generations. And they will continue to do so in your life, as you read.

Let's honor them and their legacy!

— Pastor Pasqual Urrabazo
Associate Pastor, International Church of Las Vegas

I have personally known Artur Simonyan for several decades and can testify that the life behind his ministry is authentic. Artur's new book, *Sisters*, is not just a theory but a very careful study of women who did amazing things with their lives and fulfilled their callings. I also personally know some of the godly ministers whose examples Artur uses in this book and can testify that everything he writes about them is true. This work is very practical and contains certain principles that every Christian should follow to fulfill God's will. I can also guarantee that this book will not only be of interest to women but also to men. I highly recommend this book to everyone!

— Rick Renner
Author, Broadcaster, Pastor

ARTUR SIMONYAN

SISTERS

DELIBRI
Moscow
2019

Sisters
Copyright © A. Simonyan, 2019
Published by Delibri, Moscow

Translator: Astghik Avetisyan

Proofreader: Bagrat Bekchyan

Editing/interior layout design by Cathy Sanders, www.csbookdesign.com.

ISBNs: 978-1-7372094-0-9 (Print)

         978-1-7372094-1-6 (Ebook)

Sisters is a series of stories of ordinary women who have done truly incredible things. They have raised their children in Soviet Union against all odds of life by edifying them in the word of God. These women were not afraid of work, they prayed diligently and they were equally faithful to their families as they were to the church. Their stories are true, simple and at the same time so touching, that it seems that you're experiencing everything written in this book together with them.

Russian Version Information:

UDC 929.5 | LBC 63.214

C37 Sisters/A. Simonyan – M.; Delibri, 2019 – 144 pages

"Who can find a virtuous wife? For her worth is far above rubies."
— Proverbs 31:10

I dedicate this book to those sisters who didn't have an abortion but rather gave birth to their amazing children, brought them up, and became role models for them.

— Artur Simonyan

CONTENTS

FOREWORD BY JOHN BEVERE

M y wife often quotes Matthew Arnold, who said, "If ever there comes a time when the women of the world come together purely and simply for the benefit of mankind, it will be a force such as the world has never known."

In over forty years of ministry, I've witnessed the emergence of women from all nations and languages who are agents of change—making a difference in their spheres of influence. Whether it's the Armenian women who have been the catalyst of the fastest growing church in the world or the stay-at-home moms who are faithfully pouring into their children—this uprising has truly been a force such as the world has never known.

In *Sisters*, my dear friend, Pastor Artur, captures a glimpse into the stories of ordinary Slavic women who are doing extraordinary things. Your faith will be strengthened by their diligence to pray, work, and remain faithful against all odds. If you've ever doubted your significance, this book will reveal how the little things, done faithfully day-in and day-out, is what ultimately makes the big difference.

— John Bevere
Best-selling Author and Minister, Co-founder of Messenger International & MessengerX

AFTER MUCH THOUGHT

I remember that amazing autumn day, when we were strolling in the city with Andrey Kochkin and his wife, conversing and looking for a place to have dinner. I was on a visit to Riga for several days and had to preach at one of the meetings in the church of these remarkable people. Please, don't think that I am trying to overpraise Andrey, no! Those who know him will definitely testify that he is a very humble person, and is a great blessing to the former Soviet Union. Andrey is known for being an anointed worshiper and preacher, but during this visit he opened up to me in a different light.

We were walking by the beautiful side-streets of the old city and we started to talk about family. I knew Andrey's sisters and most of his brothers quite well. I had never been familiar with life in a large family, and Andrey came from a big family, so I started questioning him about his childhood. My childhood seemed easy to me; I grew up in a small family, but when I grew up and gave my life to Jesus, I came to church and noticed that the majority of Christians had many children. I have always wondered what it is like to live in a large family. Is it difficult for children to live in these types of families? How are the parents able to take care of every single child, especially making sure that they remain in God? Staying on the right track is difficult. And most of the people at church had no less than four children. How do we need to bring them up? I decided to find out about all these things that evening.

"Andrey, I think your family was quite large. How were your parents able to bring you up so that all of you remained in God and most of you became ministers? Did they use any special methods? Most believers today don't have many children; some of them leave the church and the ministry is out of question," I stated. "You and your brothers not only stayed committed to God, but your lives are full of ministry and the church."

Andrey smiled. After thinking a while, he answered, "You know, I can't really name one thing in particular. The only thing I remember is that our house was always filled with guests, and every time we had to yield our beds to them."

"Every time?" I asked.

"Yes; every time."

Andrey continued talking about his family, and I started recalling my childhood. I couldn't remember a single occasion when I had to give my bed up to somebody else.

"Andrey, weren't you mad at the guests?" I asked.

"Of course we weren't. Guests were loved in our house, both by the children and by the adults. Giving up our beds to them was a habitual, and even an obligatory thing. In the evenings, we would gather for prayer, and afterward, the guests would tell stories about God's miracles. Mom cooked food in a big cooking pot so it would be enough for everyone. I and my brothers gave up our beds to the guests, and we either slept together in one bed—packed in like sardines—or on the floor wherever we found a spot to sleep."

"How interesting." It was like his words opened up my eyes. "Maybe that's why all of you remained Christians?"

"I don't know," Andrey simply answered.

That day, I questioned him for a long time about family and possible reasons for healthy relationships in it. I so much wanted to know what the key to success was. After dinner, we went to church, and during worship, a thought hit my mind that this conversation between me and Andrey was not a coincidence. I got so hooked on the topic of family that I decided to research it in more depth.

Since that day, an idea formed in my heart to find out as much as possible about the old (but not at all outdated) school of "correct parenting."

You have to understand one thing. When Andrey was growing up, his parents didn't take any Bible courses or graduate from a Christian university or seminary. The adults read the Bible, prayed with their families, and helped one another however they could. Back then, if I was told that one day we would have to persuade people from the pulpit to read the Word of God, I'm quite sure I wouldn't believe it. The main help and support in the lives of Christians was Scripture.

SISTERS

What did the people of that generation know that helped their children, despite all the difficulties, keep their faith and stay faithful and loving? What did the parents do that we missed? Had their generation achieved something valuable that is unknown to us? I think so. Having come to this conclusion, I started musing on these two questions:

1. What did they have?
2. What have we lost?

It took me seven years to examine this phenomenon. In search of an answer, I turned to different ministers who came from large families. Their answers gave birth to more questions—sometimes contradicting ones. At the beginning, I was searching for something similar in the stories of these families, but was only able to find it after several years when I was invited to preach in Yaroslavl.

I met Andrey Dirienko, the pastor of the church in which I would be ministering. I highly appreciate these types of ministers; their life involuntarily becomes an example for others. They do not need as much of that higher theological education because his close walk with the Lord is visible to others, which is the most important thing.

With just a little time before the meeting would start, I asked Andrey about his childhood. It turned out that he did not live in Russia his whole life, but was born in Kyrgyzstan into a large family. Here was another person who grew up among Christians and was brought up in a large family, not at all like my own.

"Andrey, how did your parents raise you up? What did they invest in you that modern people are missing?"

Andrey Dirienko took a deep breath, laughed, and said, "I have never thought about that."

"Please try to remember, who spent more time with you, was it your mom or dad?"

This question seemed quite simple to him. "It was mom, of course," Andrey answered without a moment's hesitation.

So the conversation turned to his mother, about how he remembered her. And at that very moment, I started to realize that sisters had right understanding of motherhood in those times. They fully devoted themselves to their husbands and children. It's amazing how a fragile woman could create a family from scratch, leaving behind such a heritage that has an influence on the whole Christian world nowadays.

At that moment I had so many thoughts that I can't name them all now. I continued my conversation with Andrey.

"Tell me, how do you remember your mom? What did she do?"

His answer surprised me very much. "My mother was very hospitable."

Hospitable? The same thing Andrey Kochkin once said about his mother. During our conversation, I highlighted for me a few principles that I could later on claim to be a key to success for these sisters and their families.

SISTERS

I am writing this book about nine women, and each of them had seven basic principles, which either they or their children spoke about, voluntarily or involuntarily, underlining the importance of them.

But before I start telling you about the lives of these mothers, let me tell you a little bit about the fathers. Their role in the family was definitely huge, but most of the time they were absent. They worked for long hours, sometimes literally "day and night" (this is understandable, a large family had to be shoed and fed, since the state was not able to provide proper assistance). And when the fathers weren't working, they were served in the army. Sometimes most of them were absent from home for a long time, arrested for their faith and were sitting in jails. Hence, the burden of caring for the family fell on the shoulders of their wives.

The women you will read about in the pages of this book have brought up and raised generations of Christians. I am not afraid to call these sisters great. Unfortunately, their principles are not highly appreciated in modern Christian families, and some of them are even despised. I can call these seven principles a weapon that helped them win the real-life battle for the lives of their children and the well-being of their families.

These women all applied the following seven principles:

1. Relentless prayers
2. Hospitality
3. Respect for father

4. Respect for the church and its ministers
5. Diligence
6. Management
7. Quality time

After noticing these principles in several stories of different families, I spent the next years asking a lot of questions and trying to find out how correct those parenting methods were.

Six months after the meeting with Andrey Dirienko, I flew to the United States of America. Leonid Malko met me at the airport. Leonid and Marina Malko are a couple who truly love God and are faithful ministers. They both grew up in large families, and I had a chance to meet with their brothers and sisters. All of them are amazing people!

When Leonid met me at the airport, we got into the car, and as we drove, I started my habitual conversation about family. Once again I got the same answers.

Unexpectedly for myself, new heroes have appeared in my heart and thoughts over the years. But these were not the typical heroes that we all know quite well, the ones with well-trained muscles and highlighted leadership abilities! These heroes are the sisters of this book.

I woke up early the next morning and Leonid was making coffee while Marina was setting the table.

The morning was beautiful, the food smelled tasty, and the conversation we were about to have promised to be exciting. This time we spoke about Marina's family. All her relatives are people of faith, I had heard confirmations of this more than once. But during my stay with Marina this time, we spoke more about her mother. Those seven principles I listed above were easily discerned in the life of this wonderful woman.

I understood that her mother was a true hero of faith. You will get to know her more while reading this book.

Andrey Kochkin, Andrey Dirienko, Leonid and Marina Malko; all of them involuntarily mentioned those seven principles that I realized are at the base of a healthy Christian family. I met many more other families and was being constantly convinced that this theory of mine was correct. These seven principles were present in the lives of many people—and were the main characteristic traits of their mothers.

After meeting with Andrey Kochkin, I realized that I was dealing with God's generals who were not popular among other people; grandmothers who raised a blessed generation of believers. This idea prompted me to write this book. My goal is to get you acquainted with the lives of these sisters who are both great and, at the same time, humble.

From time to time, I am asked the following question, "Outside the Bible, can I call someone a hero?" Of course you can, because up to this point, I had several such people that I could call heroes, but I was so happy to find new ones. They all are the sisters from the pages of this book.

How I wanted to communicate with each of these women personally! Unfortunately, I was not able to meet with every one of them. The total number of blessed women can be in the thousands, but I'll tell you about nine of them.

1. Maria Zubrilina

The first woman that I write about is sister Maria. She's ninety years old, and out of ninety, she's been praying for me for thirty years. She doesn't leave her ministry as long as you and I live, work, and serve. Maria is praying for a revival and the church for hours every day. Despite her age and weakness, she does not stop attending church. For several years, Maria has had problems with her kidneys. They don't function normally. She goes through dialysis three times a week. Even young people can't take this procedure well. She does not stop serving God for a minute.

Lusine and I interviewed Maria at the house of her daughter Vera while I was writing this story. During the recording, I asked her the following question, "What would you like to say to today's youth?"

She answered without hesitation, "Not only young people, but also children and adults should not stop praying. It's the air that we breathe, and only because of it we are alive."

I asked her a question again, "How many hours a day do you pray?"

"I spend a lot of time on my knees," Maria simply answered.

As she speaks, I think, *My God, this woman is going through a dialysis; her kidneys are not functioning well. You*

SISTERS

can even say that she is an incomplete person. And at the same time, she is ninety years old. But she does not give up, always thinking about others and crying out to God for our generation. She is a real heroine of faith!

I was touched, but I put my thoughts together and continued the interview. You will find the story of this amazing woman in the pages of this book.

2. Galina Vitalievna

I looked forward to meeting the next sister for a long time, and finally the day came. Before I would start the conversation with Galina Vitalievna, she had already made a great impact on me. I personally know some of her children and grandchildren; exemplary people, decent Christians, and anointed ministers.

Imagine a large family. One day the husband leaves them. Communism. After coming home from work, she had to take care of her ten children, feed them, bring them up, and help them as much as she could. At the same time, she had no hatred toward her husband. She passed onto her children such love and respect toward their father, which caused their father to return home many years later.

I remember well the moment we stood in front of Galina's house. She lives in Portland. Sergey Kozlov's son Dima drove me there. The door opened, and a beautiful grandmother greeted us. After the greeting, she invited us to the table. Before the meeting, me and Dima managed to eat, but time hadn't changed the hospitable character of Galina Vitalievna.

24

She cooked potatoes and different dishes, and was telling us to eat. With a great difficulty, we convinced her that we were not hungry.

But she insisted that we try her kissel. She poured a warm kissel for us, and we drank it with a great pleasure. I was holding my cup and thinking how many children, grandchildren and great-grandchildren were brought up on her kissel.

Galina made a great impression on me during our conversation. I was curious as to why she was not disappointed in her husband, because he had left them at a very decisive moment. So I asked, "Sister Galina, what can you say about your husband?"

Even though her husband was in heaven, it was surprising that Galina Vitalievna was still in love with him. She told all the good things that she remembered about her husband and the big fishes that he used to catch. But honestly, I wanted to know about the thing that bothered me the most:

"Let's leave the fishes aside for a second; tell me how were you able to accept your husband back again? He cheated on you and left you for another woman."

Once more her answer shocked me. From time to time, I meet with rejected and faithful women, and I love talking with them. But what Galina told me, I heard for the first time.

"Brother, that was not my husband's fault. The devil blinded him. A normal person would never cheat on his family. When my husband left me, I told my kids that it was not him, but the devil. Every day I kept saying that their father was good, but the devil led him into deception. Day and night, we were praying to snatch him from the claws of the devil. God told me that my husband will return, and it was as He said."

"Galina, were you able to hear God's voice?"

"Yes, of course; God told me what was going to happen and how."

I asked one more difficult question:

"Have all of your children remained Christians, or still some of them remained in the world?"

Galina named one of his sons and said, "He started to lead a secular life, but I knelt down and prayed until God told me the exact date and time of his homecoming. And at that exact date and hour, my son started believing in God, just like in good old times."

I noted with delight, "Sister, you are a prophetess!"

"Brother, I am not a prophetess." She replied humbly, "I am an ordinary woman."

On that day, I realized how the church could become rich by the experiences of such women like Galina, but this did not happen because the sisters did not share the stories of their lives with others.

When I met with the sisters of this book, I had the same feeling as if I would have met with prophets, apostles, or teachers. I think not a single Christian university would be able to give me the things that I learned from them.

Galina's story left a great impression on me. But it would be better if you read her story for yourself.

After a long conversation, we took many pictures, and afterward, I asked Galina to bless me. She prayed for me, and after bidding her goodbye, Dima and I left the house.

The whole time while we were driving the car, Dima said only one word, "Wow!"

"Dima, can you imagine how many anointed people live among us, and we don't even know about it. What kind of people filled with knowledge and wisdom are humbly sitting on the church pews, and no one even suspects it. It's out of question that their wisdom could serve well in our houses too!

The rest of the road we were silent. We both were touched and thoughtful.

3. Vera Franchuk

After a few days, I visited another sister named Vera. She is younger than the first two women and lives in a large family with her children, grandchildren, and great-grandchildren.

All of the children were gathered at Vera's house that day. A large and beautiful table was set. I immediately understood that she is hospitable too, and she welcomes guests with a great joy. As I looked into the eyes of Vera and at her children, they all radiated such light.

After talking with sister Vera, I got acquainted with her friend. She also came in to see Vera. She told me a little bit about her life. She told me that she worked at "Bolshoy" theatre in Moscow. From our conversation, I understood that she was a very well-known person.

"How did you become a believer?" I asked.

"Thanks to the way Vera conducted herself."

You will read about her story in the pages of this book as well, but about that a bit later. While communicating with women like Galina, Maria, or Vera, I was continuously thinking, *What a magnificent example they are! How come we have never heard about them?*

From the conversation with Vera, I learned something that was new for me too, something that we lost hold of; teaching about dreams. It's not widespread at church nowadays; we might even say it doesn't exist. But it exists in the lives of people, and it manifests in amazing ways, in which I became quite convinced while listening to Vera.

Moreover, today I receive thousands of e-mails from people from a Russian-speaking field, asking me to explain their dreams. I will tell you that eighty percent of those dreams are prophetic. I always ask, "Why aren't you turning to your pastor for helping you to understand your dreams?" and I mostly receive the same answer, "We did, but we were told that it's a stupid dream and we need to forget it."

One of the reasons that this phenomenon is common at church is because when we think of a preacher, we imagine someone who speaks things that are acceptable to our understanding. And little by little, we depart from the spiritual world. At the same time, there are people like Vera sitting among us in the church, but we don't even notice them! Before I continue my story about this sister, I would like to share with you another one.

Some of you may not know that my daughter Anna is in heaven. Long before her sickness manifested itself, I saw in my dream what was going to happen to her. Many times, I have witnessed how people were dying, but this time was different. I woke up crying and continued to cry.

Try as hard as I could, but I was not able to understand the meaning of that dream. Of course, I prayed and destroyed the works of the devil. However, everything happened exactly as it was in the dream.

Anna was already in heaven, but I continued asking the ministers who were coming to me, "why did God show me that dream?"

Most of my friends told me frankly that they didn't know the answer, but some of them assumed, "God was warning you in that way."

I thought exactly the same way as some of my friends, that God wanted to warn me about something, but inside there was a constant battle, and I didn't have peace. *Why did He show it to me then?* If God warned me but He was not able to do anything about it, then why did I needed to know? I searched for an answer, but wasn't able to find one.

A new world opened up to me while talking to Vera. She told me about an incident that happened to her son. The devil wanted to kill him. Vera saw in a dream how her son would die in a car crash. Her words stuck in my heart.

"I woke up and understood that the devil wanted to harm my son. So I knelt down and prayed for several days. I snatched my boy from the claws of the devil by fasting for him for a month and continuously crying out to the Lord."

"How did you know that you needed to do that?"

"Brother, nowadays nobody speaks about it, but the older sisters at church were telling the younger sisters how their dreams should be treated."

At that point I realized with sadness that we have omitted a lot. After the interview with Vera, we had a dinner and I went home. While driving, I was still thinking, *Dear Lord, give me strength and an opportunity to create a platform where I can reveal everything that these sisters knew. May be this book will become a starting point for it.*

I want to repeat the principles about which I have written at the beginning:

These sisters were hospitable, respected their husbands, prayed in spirit, and never condemned the church. They brought up their children in the spirit by making use of spiritual weapons. Each of these sisters had those qualities.

4. Maria Kozlova

My next faith hero is Maria Kozlova. The Kozlov dynasty is famous for being a dynasty of ministers. It doesn't matter whether you are in Russia or in the United States, you will definitely find a preacher with a last name Kozlov. Maria and her husband changed this world for real. They had 14 children, 11 of which survived. While alive, they saw their 70 grandchildren, 165 great-grandchildren and 26 great-great grandchildren. While I was writing the book, Maria and her husband both went to heaven. Of course, their grandchildren and great-great grandchildren will continue to multiply in number. And the impact that Maria had on her family will be spread all over the world. There are many ministers and businessmen in her generation, and all of them have amazing families. Isn't this a blessing for all of us?

I know many in Maria's family personally, and if I lived next to each one of them, I would certainly be enriched spiritually. The more I learned about her life, the more I was able to notice the strong traits of her character. Maria was very disciplined, and she taught her family to live like that by dividing the daily chores equally. The kids shared the responsibilities with her, and that's why they grew up as hard-working people. Every time I think of Maria, I have this image of a strong leader in my head. Unfortunately, there are not so many people like her in modern churches today.

If women were allowed to serve on an equal basis with men when Maria was young, she would have made an excellent administrator, and the church would have succeeded much more than it has now. But however, not so long ago, women had to keep silent, be inactive, and just pray.

Besides administrative gifts, Maria had spiritual qualities that her children inherited as well. They learned to pray, read, and study the Bible. The father of the family worked very hard, and luckily he had Maria as a real support at home during his absence.

I was so happy to meet her. Although Maria and her husband are with the Lord now, I have to be a little patient to get to know her better. Her son Sergey Kozlov tells us about his mother in the book. He is my friend and the pastor of one of the most thriving Russian-speaking churches in America.

5. Valentina Agapova

The next hero of my book is Valentina Agapova. She is with the Lord just like Maria. I went to her grave and saw her picture on the tombstone, and it seemed to me that her grave was a place where even after her death, Valentina continued to testify others about God's love and the gospel. She was smiling at me from the picture.

Like the other couples, Nikolay and Valentina had many children. Although she is no longer with us, I had a chance to speak with the son and the husband of this amazing woman.

While talking about his mother, Vladimir was hardly able to restrain himself from crying. Whenever he made a pause, he would wipe away his tears and then continue to speak. Don't think that he is a weak person. In fact, Vova is a strong, sturdy, and a well-built man. Whenever I see a man with teary eyes, I have no idea what could make him cry. In case of Vova, I see that the influence of his mother on her children was so great that they were missing her even after her death.

Valentina was a hospitable woman. She was respected at church and devoted her life to her family and God. According to her relatives, she was kind, patient, and yielding. I think she lived by the principle "Do well to others" despite of how she felt herself.

This is how I define the difference between a kind or an evil man. An evil person wants to feel good, while the other person feels bad. And the kind person does not mind feeling bad, because the most important thing is to make others feel good, which was Valentina Agapova's motto for life.

After speaking with Volodya, I met up with his father. He was an elderly man who loved God and His Word. While speaking about his wife, Nikolay wasn't able to restrain himself from crying as well.

I used to think that only God's presence and an unbearable pain could make a man cry. With great pleasure, I would have written another book by the titled, *Women Who Made the Men Cry*, after getting acquainted with these people.

The tears mean that Valentina was worthy of it all. She was very hard-working. She would take the children to kindergarten and different activities, and after that she would go to work so that her children were not in need of anything. Despite the fact that Nikolay was working too, Valentina still had to help him. According to Vladimir, their mother had a special place in the lives of her children. They helped her around the house. Their mother was a great role model for them and the examples that she set for her children touched their hearts deeply. Vova told me how his mother would give the best lumps of meat to them and their father, leaving the giblets or the lungs of the chicken for herself.

There was time when she would make dumplings for sale day and night to support the family budget.

My God, what a strong woman she was that despite multiple responsibilities, she did everything with love and patience! Everyone I talked with about Valentina said the same thing, that she loved the church very much, she liked to sing in the choir, and everyone invariably repeated that she was a hard-worker.

After the interview, I was in the car with Volodya and I asked him, "Vov, if there was a vacancy for a hero, who would you nominate?"

"My mom," he simply answered.

6. Anna Trachuk

The next hero about whom you will read in the pages of this book is Anna Trachuk. She and her husband gave birth to six sons and two daughters. Some of them are my friends. Plus, I know Anna's grandchildren very well and all of them are decent people.

Anna's son Ivan told me that their house was not far from church, and he couldn't recall any occasion when guests were not treated well in their house. The doors of their house were wide open for people, and guests never asked them for permission to stay there. It didn't matter whether they were acquaintances or total strangers, accommodation and refreshments awaited everyone.

It was a great pleasure for me to talk to Ivan; he is not only a pastor of a church, but also my good friend and a man who knows God very well.

"You haven't graduated from any biblical courses, right? Then how did you get this kind of knowledge about God and life?'" I asked—and wasn't much surprised by his answer.

"It comes from my mom."

Anna was the very element that united her family, she was constantly praying for her husband and children. What an amazing example of love! You can learn more about her from her son's story.

I found a lot of women like Anna. While studying their lives and driving through United States in search of new stories,

I thought quite a lot. And I came to the following conclusion: what an irreplaceable loss for our generation not to be able to receive instructions from these women in person.

However, it's a loss for the modern church, but not for God. The knowledge and love of women like Valentina, Galina, and Anna had passed to their children. As of today, the majority of the ministers in the Russian-speaking churches are their sons and daughters.

Although these sisters didn't have a chance to teach at church, they were able to freely speak and act in their own families. So all of their children repeat in unison, "The title of 'hero' belongs to Mom."

7. Nadezda Klimenko

While writing this book, I received a letter from a woman who had just become a Christian. It read, "Pastor, please pray for me, I can't forgive myself. I have beaten my three-year-old child to an extent of losing consciousness."

I read that terrible letter and started to think. At that time, I was working on Nadezda Klimenko's testimony, a mother to nineteen children. According to her daughter, their mother had neither raised her voice to them nor had beaten them. She served as an example and a role model for how her children should conduct themselves, and because of that, all of them remained at church.

Here we have two testimonies that allow us to see the difference between people; first, we have a mother who beats her child to death, and on another hand, we have a mother who gives birth to nineteen children and brings them up in love. Some people believe in God, and some people don't. The strength of a woman comes from God, and one can discern this by looking at their fruits.

I remembered a program that day on Animal Planet which marked a very important detail for me: a lion never beats its cub. A lion shows its cub how things need to be done.

Let us be good examples for our children. And when they grow up in our likeness, we will be filled with joy and not disappointment.

8. Maria Samolyich

In the process of writing the book, I met up with another good friend, Slava Samuilovich. He is in a pastoral ministry in Massachusetts. Slava is one of those people that you want to be next to all the time, his job is to restore and strengthen churches.

I asked him the same question, "Who is your mom for you?"

"My mom is my Bible school, my spiritual university, my teacher, and my hero."

What more can I add to these words?

Women like the ones from this book, are true treasures that one needs to seek for. In Proverbs 31 it's written, "*Who* can find a virtuous wife?" Only now have I come to understand why the word *who* is accentuated here.

This type of women can be found only at church. Unfortunately, people look for a virtuous woman in movies, among the actresses, photo models, and famous people; they look up to them and their lifestyle. Of course, it's possible to find a wife among these women, but hardly a virtuous one.

Being a virtuous woman is a gift that God gives the ones who read and act upon the Word of God.

I dedicate this book to all those sisters and women who do not place their value in self-care in beauty salons, or how they look like when they see themselves in the mirror, or converse with their friends sitting in the cafes, but the ones who gave their lives to their families, children, and God.

MARIA ZUBRILINA

I don't like to talk much about myself, but if you're asking, I will share my memories about marriage and faith with you.

I recently turned ninety. My husband and I had ten children. We have even more grandchildren and great-grandchildren, and our family consists of one hundred people today.

SISTERS

No, I don't consider myself a hero. I simply lived and believed in God and had the fear of God in me. For instance, my husband, Andrew, was revered as a holy man, and I am just an ordinary woman.

I will tell you a little bit about my youth. My family adhered to the Orthodox faith. Since childhood, my mom injected God's fear in us (in other words, respect toward God). I spent all my childhood praying on my knees in front of the symbols of our religion. When the war began, we all wanted one thing—for it to end as soon as possible, and for all our fathers and grandfathers to return home.

I prayed with all my heart and without showing off. I remember deciding that I was not leaving the house without receiving a blessing. I believed that God would protect me. Those were very difficult years for us, but my mom was lucky to have four helpers at home. Her four daughters helped her a lot around the house.

A young girl moved to Abkhazia with her sister, sister's husband, and uncle in 1948. After a while, my uncle and I stayed alone because my sister decided to return. There wasn't much to be done in my native land, so I decided to get a profession and get my life back together.

I got a job in a cafeteria as a dishwasher, and a little later, I graduated from canteen worker courses and got a new position. I met my husband while working in the cafeteria. Andrey was the driver of the cafeteria's director. That's how he noticed me.

Andrey usually asked permission from my uncle to date me. And if my uncle allowed me to meet him, we would go to the movies. This is how our friendship started. I remember Andrey once asked me, "Do you believe in God?" I answered that I do believe in God, of course.

But at that time, people were like savages; they could do such things that I don't even want to talk about. They were fearless and not able to discern what was good and what was bad.

And I asked my future husband what it meant for him to "know the truth." He simply answered that his parents were spiritual people, and that they know.

"How can you understand if your parents are spiritual or not?" I was surprised.

"How? They prayed and received Jesus Christ in their hearts."

"I believe in Jesus because I am an orthodox Christian," I objected to him without even understanding.

"Your faith is not right; you worship idols."

"How come?" I asked in bewilderment. The meaning of his words was revealed to me after a while.

It turned out that we started living together. Yes, we didn't arrange a wedding. We had a contemporary way of thinking or, in more simple words, a secular way of thinking. But when we moved to my husband's relatives in

SISTERS

Kodori, my life opened up to me in a different light. I got acquainted with his whole family; Andrey had brothers and sisters too. We stayed there for a while, and they blessed us with various gifts and things. I was not used to such treatment. There was poverty and devastation everywhere, but their family was very generous to us.

One evening after dinner when everyone was gathered in one room, Andrey's brothers and sisters sang a hymn.

To this day, I still remember the lines to the song: "To an unearthly land a path is shown to me and something keeps me moving forward all the time," I cried so hard. I was thinking, "God, I am such a sinner, and they are so holy." I used to think that holy people were elderly men living in peace with everyone. It felt like the heavens descended, and I felt so good that I wanted to stop doing anything secular. *I should be cleansed from all the vanity and sin*, I thought.

I so much loved to hang out with my friends before, to go out dancing or watch movies. But when I got to know my husband's relatives, I was constantly asking God, "Please deliver me from all these whims and have mercy on me." From that day on, I stopped hanging out with secular friends.

I still remember 1949 and the times of Communism. That system didn't terrify us much because things were a lot more peaceful in our small village in Caucasus than in any other big city in Russia. The only thing that I remember is that Baptists were being persecuted everywhere because they were secretly printing out their brochures and distributing them. Of course, they were being exposed and put in jail. But luckily, we escaped imprisonment. Someone could simply mock our faith, but they wouldn't do anything bad for it.

Aftere we got married, I gave birth to Andryusha. We didn't have our own house in Abkhazia, but thanks God, my husband had a job, and we had enough money. I recall those days with great warmth in my heart; I became acquainted with believers who were my peers. They were Pentecostals. They were carpenters who came over there to find a job.

My husband and I were renting a room, and not far from it was a barrack. Sasha Shovikov, Petya Novikov, and his sister settled in the barrack. If I am not mistaken, Sasha was already married back then. But the most important thing for me was that they were believers.

On Sunday morning, we were talking to them in the street when I noticed Nadya washing the clothes on the side. People adhering to orthodox faith don't do any chores on Sundays. That surprised me a lot, and I thought, "Why is she committing such a sin?" I was taught that way. Not being able to restrain from asking, I said, "Don't you know that today is Sunday? Why are you sinning in vain?"

"Do you even believe in God?" asked Nadya, grinning.

"Maybe I believe more than you do," I answered boldly.

SISTERS

Such were my ideas about faith. Everybody respected Andrey, and I might even say they were a little bit afraid of him because they considered him holy. God's fear restrained me from committing stupid things, I gave birth to ten children, and all of them believe in God. I wish everyone was the same. But my neighbors used to laugh at me and say:

"What do you need so many children? Why do you keep having them?"

"The road to senility will be gratifying," I would boldly answer to all my friends who didn't believe in Jesus.

And now my beloved ones take such good care of me. I tell them not to buy new clothes for me anymore because I am old and won't be able to wear them all, but they won't stop. They say, "We want you to look beautiful!"

We didn't need anything even before. My husband was working day and night, and I was taking care of the children at home. If the children didn't complete the chores around the house, they wouldn't go to the sea. First, they needed to complete the house chores and only then go for a walk. The orchard, the vegetable garden, the cows, and the geese would not wait until evening. Since our household was not small, there was enough work for everyone. That was the main reason everyone was fed and not hungry.

Whenever we had guests, our chores doubled. But this wasn't a problem; we were able to figure out how to feed them and make space for everyone to sleep. In the summer,

44

the children were sleeping in the barn because there was a lot of hay, and it was warm and spacious. During the colder months we were still receiving guests, even though the house was a little bit crowded.

Our guests were mainly believers coming from various parts of the world like Siberia, Ukraine, or Vilnius. The local parish would give visitors our address, and they would come over to our house, knocking on our door with the following words, "Hello. We were given your address. Will you accept us?"

We never said no to anyone. When our son Slavik returned home from the army, we started having even more guests, especially when he got acquainted with his future wife, Tanya.

I cooked absolutely everything. I made pierogi and dumplings. As soon as I prepared the breakfast, it was high time to make something for lunch and dinner.

I always talked with my children about God. We loved more to communicate with one another. That was why I usually gathered them for prayer and shared the gospel with them. On Sundays we went to church with our whole family.

For me, it didn't matter how old the child was; I never waited for them to grow up to talk about God. I taught my children to pray at an early age. Andrey even told me that I shouldn't try so hard, that I need to leave them alone.

But I gently objected him, trying not only to pray for my children but also to sow truth in their hearts.

Andrey was a good husband and father; he always helped me around the house. He had one very special characteristic trait—compassion. If he was aware of the need of someone's family, he would never remain indifferent to it. Whatever was necessary for that family, he would take it to them ahead of us, leaving his family in expectation for couple more days. As soon as he received his salary, he would find out the needs of those in the church and buy potatoes and sugar for everyone, for instance. But this didn't upset anyone in our family; everyone felt dad's love and understood that it was the right thing to do.

Maybe that was the reason why people considered him a saint. He was kind, generous, and hard-working. Christians often came to our house after imprisonment for rehabilitation. My husband himself accepted them and took care of them as if they were his own family. He made sure that their health was being restored, and he gave them homemade natural juice to drink. Although these people came to us broken, sometimes homeless, and after a long separation from their relatives, I had never heard them complain. It was not acceptable in our house to condemn the actions of the government or church ministers; we thought more about God's miracles and spoke more about his great mercy.

A minister, a grandpa from the Kozlov family, stayed with us for some time as he recovered from imprisonment. When he started to feel better, it was time for him to return home. After saying farewell, the grandpa went to the train station. A few seconds after he left the house, Andrey decided to go after him and bless him with money. He was right on time. It turned out that the grandpa didn't have money to buy a ticket, and he was ashamed to ask us. My husband gave him the amount of money to buy the ticket, and the grandpa was so happy.

"Andrey, I stood here and prayed. I had no money for the trip."

After these words, they bid farewell, and the grandpa walked to the ticket window.

As much as the money blessed the grandpa, we were blessed even greater. We all admired God's providence and the fact that our dad knew how to hear God's voice.

So many years have passed since then. My children have all grown up and departed; but most importantly, they did not leave the church, and they all believe in God. My only prayer to Jesus in the mornings was the things I named in the previous sentence. I prayed for God's protection over my family and for blessing over the church. Even now, I continue to pray for the people around me, and for our nation so everyone will be able to know God's love.

All my prayers were about my children when they were little. I gave them into the hands of God every day. But these times are different. When the night falls, I have no time for sleep because I have to take over the night watch. I usually pray for the preachers of the Lord to bless them and encourage them and give them spiritual strength during their meetings. I pray for that power to expand to all the members of the church.

In my nineties, I am free to pray not only for the concerns of my family, but for the concerns of others too. If the ministers are strong in the Spirit of God, God can do a lot of things through them, like melting the human hearts from unbelief.

As for me, I am loved and surrounded by the warmth of my relatives. This is my happiness.

GALINA KONKINA

I am an orphan. I was brought up by my stepmother. I was ten months old when my mother died. After a while my dad died too. I grew up in difficult times, and sometimes I was so hungry that I had to steal food. I stole bread and sugar. Many of you probably don't understand what it's like to be hungry all the time.

Before I was born, my dad studied at zoo-technical university in Moscow, and after graduating, he was sent to Kalmykia and stayed in Elista. I was born there, and after their death, I lived there.

I remember a time when I was eleven years old. It was November, and my girlfriends and I were playing hide-and-seek. It was dark and cold. We loved to hide in the hay. There was a lot of hay not far from my home, and we used to play until late at night.

Suddenly, I heard my stepmother's voice calling me, "Alla, come here!" That's my real name. When my documents were drawn up, my stepmother not only changed my name, but also reduced my age so that I would receive compensation for my father, who died at the front.

I ran home and asked her, "Mom, did you call me?"

"No, I told you I haven't called you," she answered from the couch.

After a while I hear my mother's voice, so persistent. "Come here."

I ran home and asked again, "Mom, did you call me?"

"Why am I stuck with you? I haven't called you!" she insisted.

"How come?" I was surprised. "I heard you call me."

I ran into the street again, and we continued to play. But I heard mom calling me by name for the third time. I turned to my girlfriends and asked, "Did you hear that my mom was calling me?"

"What are you saying?" they said. "No one is calling you."

I was afraid so much that when the time came to hide, I ran far away. The voice was so real that it definitely seemed to me that someone was calling me. I fell on my knees, looked at the sky, and it felt as if an electric shock passed through me. It was so powerful. I was not able to understand what was going on with me back then. I was shaking, I kept looking at the sky and thought, *This is not some kind of an symbol, this is the living God.* And He was calling me; He was calling me by name.

My girlfriends started calling out to me, and I was not able to come back to my senses after what I had experienced. I came out of my hideout only when everyone was gone home, and I went home too. Mom was fast asleep, and I silently crawled underneath my blanket. I wanted to sleep, rest a little bit, but I couldn't. I kept thinking about what happened to me. Tears were rolling down my cheeks. From that moment on, I had a great desire to pray with all my heart. I kept sinning like before, of course; however, the moment when I knelt down and said the daily prayer and repented of everything that I did wrong during the day was very important to me.

I grew up like that. After graduating from the seven-year school, I left for Astrakhan to become an accountant. But I failed the exams. It was sad to return home. What could I do?

SISTERS

That year, courses for livestock breeders were first opened in Elista. I enrolled in those courses, studied for ten months, and after that I was allocated to Dzhakuevka, Primorsky state farm of the Astrakhan region. I was sent there as an assistant to the veterinarian. Maria, the sister of my future husband, Vanya, worked there. She was the chief veterinarian and the head of the pharmacy. We were friends.

I was still that mischievous girl. I asked for a leave from work to go to the cinema with my girlfriends, doing anything I could to go. My mother was very religious and did not approve this hobby.

Sometimes we were taken to a karakul-breeding state farm, seventeen kilometers away from where we lived; they didn't have enough specialists there. Despite the flocks of sheep that were waiting for us, there were many other breeds of animals as well.

I will never forget the fleas and the lice. I would run to the barchans, strip down my clothes, and stay in my underwear to kill all the fleas, but these disgusting creatures seemed to attack me by the hundreds. When I returned home, the first thing I did was run to the bathroom, take off my clothes, quickly wash off all the dirt and the remaining insects, and then I washed my clothes thoroughly and ironed them well. This process was repeated time after time. The lice were dying, but the nits weren't hatched yet—and even the hot boiling water was not able to kill them all! I fought them as best as I could.

I was an ordinary girl living among the Kazakhs, even though I had the fear of God in my heart. They tried to rape me three times in a row. Oh, I was so young and not experienced.

One day, one of them asked me, "Let's go over to my house; the calf is sick. I need your help."

I believed him and went to his house. He was riding on the horse, and because there was no other horse for me I had to go through the barchans on foot. After three to four kilometers, he got off of the horse and started pestering me so badly that I screamed. I started praying to God, "Please, have mercy on me, save me, Lord." At that moment, the legs of the Kazakh got tangled in the bridle of the horse, and that saved my life.

I ran all the way home, and I was not able to catch my breath. Since then, I stayed away from males. I became smarter.

I worked as a nurse for two years, but I wanted to attend a college so much that I decided to try once more. It might sound funny, but I failed the Russian language exam. During the war, we tried to escape from hunger in North Ossetia, and the school program was two years behind from the actual curriculum in those places. That was the reason that I didn't master the Russian language as well as I should have. I went back to work upset.

Vanya came to the farm to get acquainted with me several times, but he wasn't able to get hold of me because I worked in the prairie at that point.

Meanwhile, Maria told me more than once, "If you marry my brother, I would be so happy. My Vania grew up in a family of believers, but over time, he walked away from the Lord.

That evening, when I returned from my exams crying all over the place, he was on the farm again, hoping to get to know me. We went to the cinema with him. I remember how Vanya said, "I'm taking you away."

"Taking me where?"

"I will tell you later. Don't be afraid. Nobody knows you are here."

When we lied down to sleep that night, I was kind of suffering. I didn't want to go anywhere. But I heard a voice inside me telling, "You will go!"

The next morning, we went straight to Astrakhan on a river bus. No, I did not leave for Astrakhan with thoughts about marriage. I wanted to relax; that was why I allowed myself to have a little vacation. But the truth is that while we were having a rest, Vanya persuaded me to marry him.

We got married and Vanya introduced me to his parents. That was how we started our family life. Vanya decided to build a house behind his parent's house. The most interesting thing for me was that while I was looking around his parent's house, I noticed that they had neither religious symbols or a cross hanging anywhere on the walls.

My mother-in-law was a very kind woman. She suggested that I read the Bible. There was a priest who had given them a Bible as a present. She handed it to me and started to pray for God to reveal Himself to me.

I obeyed my mother-in-law and started reading the Bible. But as soon as I would open the book to read, someone would knock on the window so hard that the glass was clinking. I would run out into the yard and ask, "Who is there?" But all I received in response was silence. Whenever I read other books, I had no uninvited guests came knocking at my window. But as soon as I started reading the Bible, I heard someone knocking at my window again. Sometimes I would shake from fear, but I didn't tell Vanya or his mother about this. However, after a month, I couldn't hold it inside anymore, and I told everything to my mother-in-law.

She taught me the following: "Whenever you hear someone knocking at your window, don't run out into the street. Kneel down and say, 'Get behind me, devil, in the name of Jesus. I served you once, but I serve the Lord now.' After declaring these words, sit down, read the daily prayer, and he will flee."

I started reading the Word from that day on. Having revealed God in the Word, I repented from all my sins. We started going to the houses of the believers where meetings were taking place.

We weren't accepted in those meetings for a long time. My husband could go drinking after payday, and he smoked sometimes. To put it simply, he was contaminated with worldly things. My mother-in-law said, "Pray for him, and everything will change."

I started praying. Sometimes Vanya came home and invited me to the movies, but I refused to go.

"I will not go anymore."

As much as I liked to have fun, I gave up my old habits.

"How are we going to live together now?" Vanya asked me.

"I want to serve the Lord. If I serve God, I have to serve Him genuinely."

Although I continued to pray for my husband, everything remained the same. One day, Vanya woke me up in the middle of the night and said, "Run to Vasya's house and don't pay attention that it's late. Tell him that I want to see him, and he will come."

"Vanya, it's two in the morning. Where shall I go?" I begged him to stay.

"Go!"

I could do nothing, so I ran to Vasya's house. Vasya put his clothes on and came with me.

On seeing his older brother, Vanya rushed to him and said, "Vasya, I can't lead a double life anymore. I want to repent."

He fell on his knees and started to pray. At that moment, God restored the gift of the Holy Spirit to Vanya.

From that day on, our life changed; we started going to the meetings at the Baptist church. Everything was very smooth and nice until the moment when Vanya's uncles started preaching about the Holy Spirit. Then we were cast out from the church.

We were left without a pastor, so we started gathering in our house. We prayed for God to send us a leader. After a while, God sent us three ministers and showed through them that Vanya's father had to become our senior pastor.

"Brothers, I'm illiterate. What am I going to say when I am not even able to instruct others?" Vasily Rodionovich objected.

"If God has chosen you, then everything will be fine. He is never mistaken. Your job is to start and finish the meeting and to choose a preacher," the ministers encouraged him.

That was how Vanya's father became our leader. The church decided to fast and pray at two o'clock in the morning. Vanya and I lived poorly. We had a clock in our house, but its alarm was not working, and there was no one to ask for money from to repair it. So, I prayed, "Lord, please wake me up. I beg You."

Every time, God woke me up, either through a voice, a noise, or sounds of the bells. I woke up at around two o'clock in the morning every day. And what a prayer that was! I can't describe it with words.

Our life with Vanya was simple but not difficult, and we had to work a lot. We had six children, and later twenty-four grandchildren, and thirty-six great-grandchildren were born to us. I might not remember the names of all my great-grandchildren, but I keep in mind the names of my grandchildren. As for the birthdays, sometimes I forget them.

In my bedroom, I have a calendar where I have written down all the names and birthdays of my grandchildren. Sometimes I call to congratulate them on their birthdays either in advance or a day later. Well, sometimes I just call them after a week and say: "Well, my dears, forgive me that I forgot to call you."

I usually started my mornings by putting the kettle on the stove, and by the time it started boiling, I read the Word of God. I was reading it alone because I was the one to wake up and leave the house early. In the evenings, we usually studied the Bible, prayed, and talked about God. But my special time with God was in the mornings.

My children read the Bible themselves as well, but not much. We went to the meetings altogether, and it didn't matter whether the children were little or if they understood the sermon or not.

My daughter Tanya received an Octobrist badge when she went to school. When she came home, she said to me enthusiastically, "Mom, look what they gave me! They didn't take any money for it." I accurately took the badge, wrapped it up in a handkerchief, and asked her to give it back.

The next day, her teacher, Tamara Ephrimovna (her father was shot in the times of Stalin), called me to school and said, "What do you think you are doing?"

SISTERS

"Tamara Ephrimovna, when you take your child to the movies, he sits next to you. Later, he will choose which movie he likes more. So when I go to church, I take my children with me. When Tanya grows up, she will decide what she wants to do. But as she is little now, I am in charge of her."

Well, Tanya withstood both being a pioneer and Komsomol. The director of the school was trying to dissuade her, saying, "Don't listen to those old wive's tales," he said, hitting his wrist hard on the table.

Tanya asked him, "Do you want to make me a Komsomol by force? I have thought about becoming a Komsomol, and I can tell you for sure that I won't become one, so please don't force me."

All of my children withstood the system. All of them studied at school without becoming an octobrist, a pioneer, or a Komsomol.

When my husband left us, things became harder for my children and me. There was a constant battle going on within me. Not recently, Vanya was a believer taking an active part in church life. He was so smart! He could gather all the young people and tell them about God. I was so happy because I prayed to God for sending me young people who would grow up to be believers.

But the enemy had detected my Achilles' heel. Vanya departed from God,…Two of my sons were serving in the army at that point; Vitya was eleven, Volodya was fifteen, and Alla was thirteen.

"God, please," I was crying, "I can't live like this anymore. I can't take this anymore."

You may be wondering why my husband left us. We had a wonderful life with my husband while we lived poorly. Then he started to earn a lot of money when he dealt with gold, and out of the blue, another woman appeared in his life. What did she want from Vanya? She wanted his money, not him.

I'm not judging my husband. My children had a hard time putting up with their father's betrayal, but I continued to repeat the same thing over and over again when I spoke to my children: "Our father is a good person. He behaves himself like this because of sin. Once and for all, remember, you don't have another father, and there won't be. He cared for us with his whole heart before he sinned."

I asked the Lord to return my husband back to his family. I even sent a letter to Vanya's oldest brother Nikolay, hoping that at least he would influence Vanya to come back home.

The next morning, I woke up, and I remember how a voice inside my head said the following, "Why you put your hope in people? They won't help your husband; only God can help him." From that day on, I stopped asking our family members to talk sense into my husband.

However, the enemy continued to persecute me with tormenting questions: "How are you going to handle this alone? Soon your sons will return from the army; what are you going to do then? How are you going to feed them all?"

I had always been strong physically. Since my children were growing up, I had to feed them more. Therefore, I was able to plant 1,200 seedlings of tomatoes at one time. Oh, how they helped me out! I paid off my debts, dressed, and prepared children for school with the money I received from selling the tomatoes. I also bought two bags of flour, potatoes, and cabbage. Oh, I just remembered that we had two pigs.

I raised my children in God's love, but at some point, apart from Volodya and Alla, my other children didn't want to walk in the Lord either. They grew up, made their choices, and left the church. But I did not give up. I cried out to God in prayer, asking Him to bring my children back to Him again. I prayed for my husband as well, but instead of praying for him to return home, I was praying his salvation.

I received a word from God that said, "He will return, and you will see him." I also received several prophecies for my family, which said, "What are you crying for? Your children are My children."

I can't even describe with words how merciful God is toward me. He showed His grace to me so many times! I saw God's helping hand in my life every day.

By that time, our son Andrey returned from the army. I noticed that he drank and smoked from time to time. One evening Andryusha was going on a date, and I asked him, "When will you come home?"

"Why, what's wrong, Mom?"

"I won't be able to sleep until you come home," I answered.

"Why is that?" Andryusha asked, surprised.

"Because I am a mother. Look around; murders and other terrible things are happening all around, so how can I sleep when you are not at home?"

"Okay, Mom! I will come home at eleven."

He was not home at eleven or midnight and not even one in the morning. After a while, I heard the wicket-gate open, and Andrey stealthily entered the house like a thief, for me not to hear that he had come home.

I called him out from the porch, "Andrey!"

"You're not sleeping?" sighed my son.

"Of course not. How can I sleep?"

Although the next night Andrey promised to come home early, everything repeated. Only this time, he came home at three o'clock in the morning. I was not able to sleep; therefore, when Andrey peeped into the room, he found me on my knees.

Casting a glance in my direction, he took the cigarettes out from his pocket, threw them into the boiler, and said, "Mom, I am giving you my word; I will not continue to live like this. I will go to the meetings with you."

Before going to bed, he asked me to wake him up early, so he didn't oversleep. I was the first one to wake up in the morning. The rain was knocking at the window. I thought, *Now, the enemy will prompt him not to go to church.* And it happened exactly the way I thought it would!

"Andryusha, you asked me to wake you up."

"Mom, where should I go? It's raining outside."

"Seriously," I said, "this doesn't even look like rain. Throw on a raincoat, and let's go."

My son got dressed and was about to pull up his boots when Nikolay returned from the night shift. He didn't go to church at that time; he departed from God.

"Where are you going at this early hour?"

"I am going to the meeting."

"What did you just say?"

I was thinking, *Lord, is it really true that Andryusha is coming with me to the meeting, not by his will?*

We arrived at the meeting, and he sat in the back row. The first preaching finished, and then the second one started. I didn't understand how it happened, but Andryusha repented and found his way back to God.

God was not only working with my heart, but He was bringing my children back to their senses. One day I opened the Bible, and my eyes read the following words, "Have not seen the just forsaken, nor his seed seeking bread." I thought, *My God, it turns out I have been a Christian for thirty years, but as I can see, I am not a believer at all. You feed the birds of the sky; why can't You feed my children?* I fell on my knees and prayed. God healed me. I have to say that my nerves were so worn out at that point that I couldn't bring even a glass of water to my mouth without spilling it. I could hardly endure the commute from home to work. And at that very moment, God touched me and healed me.

I saw a dream again after a while, and God spoke to me, saying, "The time has come, your children will come back to you. I will start with Nikolay, the oldest one of your sons."

I jumped out of my bed and ran to my relatives early in the morning.

"Yura, Nadya!" I exclaimed happily from the porch. "The Lord will bring Nikolay back to Him."

"That's nonsense, Aunt Galya. I saw him in the pub yesterday."

"Don't you dare to break my faith," I answered and left.

SISTERS

After a short period of time, a discord broke out in Kolya's family. I was in complete despair. But once one of the believers met my son and told him, "Kolya, I look at you and see that you don't hold your cigarette the same way as non-believers do. We have water baptism tonight, will you come?

"Why should I go? I'm not even a member of the church."

But he went to church with this brother anyway. During the water baptism on ice, Kolya turned to God and repented. He found the door to his house closed when he came home.

"Marina, Marinochka," Kolya was calling out for his wife. She let him in, I don't know the details, but Koly repented wholeheartedly, and they reconciled. The next day, he came to church to ask for forgiveness from God in front of the whole congregation. He got baptized after two months. On Easter, after his brother, Vitya was the next to repent, and now it was my eldest daughter Tanya's turn.

After long wanderings, Tanya found her way back to the Lord, so all my children are Christians now. All of them have found their way to God; however, the path wasn't an easy one.

As for my husband, I was waiting for him to return home because I believed in God, and He gave me a word, do you remember? I had to nurture that word.

I prepared my children for meeting with their father so they wouldn't judge him. I think Vanya came home the moment when each of my children forgave their father in their hearts and were spiritually ready for his return. He came home seventeen years later, and we lived as one family as if nothing had happened.

I didn't think that the new life with Vanya would start with migration, but it was what it was.

My daughter Alla had to move to America. Shortly before that, I allowed her to go to Caucasus, Cherkesssek. When Alla told me she was going to move overseas, I was very surprised and said, "How? The Lord is leading you out, and what about us?"

I was in despair again, but my sufferings didn't last long. I asked the Lord why these things were happening in our lives and did a three-day fast. I heard a voice on the third night, "I will lead you out like Lot." Since that day, I calmed down and began to wait for the fulfillment of the promise.

The documents for my daughter and her family were ready, and now they had to wait for the invitation. Before their departure, I couldn't hold it back anymore, so I told her, "I don't know when the Lord will lead me out, but I believe in His words. Soon I will move out from here too."

Here's how it all happened. My husband received his documents, and he left for America with our eldest son. I lived with my youngest son and, together with his family, migrated later than anyone else. What was interesting was that all Astrakhan residents were granted a refugee status, but I was granted a status according to which a person is temporarily deprived of the privileges of the refugee status, but they still could stay in the country. I came to the States with little money in my pocket. I didn't take anything with me. So that's what the words of the Lord "as Lot will lead you out" mean.

When I was praying about moving out of the country, I used to think this way, *If they grant me a refugee status, then I won't be able to live with my husband again. I will have to live separately.* But Lord arranged everything differently. I fulfilled my promise and lived with my husband for twenty-five years in America, after which he went to be with the Lord.

What more can I say? Our life was filled with God's miracles. My job was to trust Him. I'll tell you about it a little bit.

I remember quite well when we were organizing Andrey's wedding but didn't have enough money for that. Feeding 350 people is a big deal! I prayed and asked God how I could make my guests happy. While I was praying, God put in Andrey's cousin's heart to go to Kalmykia and buy meat.

I was so grateful to him. I cooked five buckets of potatoes with meat and five buckets of pilaf out of twenty-seven kilograms of beef. All the guests were fed, and we had some food left for the second day as well. See, these types of miracles happened!

I had never seen heaven in my dreams, but one day the wife of Vanya's brother had a car crash and died. Her ten children stayed motherless, and I remember how I was praying. I was weeping to God, saying, "Why did this happen, Lord? It would be better if you took me instead of her. What are they going to do now?"

The Lord's response to my prayer was terrifying, but He didn't take His mercy away from me.

After the funeral, my legs refused to obey me, I lost my speech, and it seemed that someone was squeezing my chest. I was suffocating, and we had to call the ambulance every now and then. Andryusha took me over to their house. I was not feeling good, and the ambulance would come three or four times a day just to do an injection.

One day I saw a dream. In my dream, I died and was able to see my body. There was a car with a coffin inside parked not far, and I was inside the coffin. The believers were singing funeral hymns and were taking the coffin to the pit. They brought the coffin down into the pit; I understood what was going on but wasn't able to say anything.

SISTERS

Suddenly, I saw a light in the distance and started walking toward it. I saw my aunt Polya on my way and hugging her I asked, "Aunt Polya, do you feel good here?"

"I do."

"Then, I will stay with you."

"No, another place is prepared for you," she said and led me along.

We walked out into a greenhouse, where a place was prepared for planting orchids. There was a big bathtub on the soil! It was filled with gravel, and a half-empty bag lay at the top.

Aunt came up to the bathtub and picked up an unequal number of stones, "Do you see what I am doing?"

"Of course, I do."

"As I said, another dwelling place is prepared for you."

When I began to come back to my senses after the dream, I sent my daughter-in-law to the ministers' meeting because I thought that the Lord wanted to take me to heaven.

The ministers started praying for my healing, refusing to let me go like Larisa, who died not long ago. That night when my daughter-in-law came back from the meeting, God healed me. I was able to walk around the room without anybody's help. I can tell you more about life and God's miracles, but I would like to keep some of them to myself.

I am happy. I can't imagine my life without God. My life with God is good and peaceful. As I became a believer, I walked with God from that day on, not doubting that I would receive an answer to all my prayers sooner or later.

I have never considered myself a strong minister of God because I am a woman. But what can I say? I am a woman of prayer.

"I loved you and your generations." These were the words of the Lord addressed to me. I don't know what did I do to deserve that kind of love. I am an ordinary woman, not a saint. Sometimes I sin a lot but repent quickly. I don't hold grudges against anybody. I can't imagine my life without God and prayer. And I want to tell you, "Children, hold tightly onto God. Serve God sincerely, and don't lead a double life, either for your parents or for the sake of showing off."

Vladimir, the son of Ivan and Galina

Not a single day passed by without having guests in our house. The table may not have looked good, but the food set on the table was very tasty and nutritious. I often found my mother in the kitchen, standing next to the sizzling pan and praying. She would always start her prayer with the following words, "Great, all-wise, almighty God," while simultaneously flipping over something in the frying pan.

My mother used to pray for my brothers and sister, and she lived to see the day when all of them found their ways back to God. Though my mother didn't allow alcohol in her house, she treated the wayward children of God with warmth and love, trying to be friends with them, not as sinners. There was not a slightest hint of condemnation from her; instead, she just prayed and believed that each of them would find their way back to God sooner or later.

My mother is a hero for me and my wife. When my father left us, it was a very painful experience for my mother in the first place—it was an unbearable pain. She loved my father very much. She never said a single bad word toward him—no matter how hard it was for her.

Many years have passed from the day when our father left us, but my mother always repeated, "If accepting Vanya back into the family will save his soul, then I will do it."

The way she treated my father became a great example for my family too. Whatever happens between the parents, they shouldn't involve their children into their personal conflicts. That's when peace will reign in the family.

Understand me right. I agree that my mom prayed a lot for me, and that's very important, but I also am grateful to my father for the best masculine qualities that he had invested in me.

Thanks to my mother, year later, my father was able to bless me and my wife and our family. I am so glad that she served as a good example for me not to scold anyone, but to have the fear of God, realizing that the Lord reigns over all of us.

VERA FRANCHUK

My name is Vera Nikolayevna Franchuk, and I am fifty-nine years old. My husband and I raised eleven children, just like my mother did, and now we have the same number of grandchildren.

I remember that I used to run to church from the time when I was eight years old. To not be late, I used to rush to the church meetings immediately after school. Neither sin nor the world was made known to me.

I got married when I was barely nineteen years old. That was when life's difficulties began. I became severely sick after my first child was born. In search of healing, I came to a church in Korosten. It was 1979. God healed me, and I remember how I asked Him the following question back then, "God, why are you treating me this way?" The answer was simple, "The time will come, and you will understand."

I got sick again after four months when my fourth child, Paul, was born. I was very sick. The doctors said it was osteo-myelitis of the bone; the bone marrow was infected. I stayed in the hospital for two weeks, even though the diagnosis was not confirmed yet. I returned home, and after a month, I was admitted to the hospital again. This time I was diagnosed with bone cancer or "bone tuberculosis," as I was told back then. While my husband, Petya, was trying to get my medication from overseas, my mother told me that when she was praying, she received a word from God that it was neither tuberculosis nor cancer, but that everything was for the glory of God.

It was very hard for me. I suffered in the hospital for two months. I remember those days with a shudder. Even so, I recovered. When I was discharged from the hospital after the treatment, the doctors bid me goodbye with the following words, "In two years, the disease will manifest itself again, and you will come back to us for treatment."

I was horrified to hear them say that. I didn't want to go through all that again! But they turned out to be right. After two years, I became as thin as a stick and was not able to eat anything. The disease had returned.

I asked Petya to go to sister Dasha, one of the prophetesses living in Vinnytsia district. When she came to me, she said boldly, "You can be healed right now, but I want you to serve the Lord. Do it with all your heart. If you are ready for this, I will pray for you." Of course, I agreed and promised her that I would serve the Lord.

Petya received another word from God on our way home, saying, "You need to go to America, otherwise there will be separation, and you will cry for long lonely days."

God healed me, and Petya didn't want to go to the States anymore. All of our relatives were going to move to the States, but Petya stubbornly refused and slowed things down. However, after a while, we moved to the States. There was a long road ahead. First, we found ourselves in Austria and stayed there for a month. Afterward, we moved to Italy and stayed there for four months. A few months before the journey, I got sick again. When we came to America, I was so ill that I felt as though I was barely alive.

I can remember it all like it happened yesterday. On the 20th of March, we arrived in the States, and my operation was scheduled for the 30th. When the doctors admitted me to the hospital they gave no hope that I would stay alive because my blood was infected, and I could barely live three days. I was on the verge of death.

God led me through a very difficult path. The only thing I heard during that time while praying to God was that I would understand everything later. Everything happened just as God said. Years have passed, but I still continue to pray constantly, realizing God's mercy and love, asking for His help and protection for my whole family.

March 30, 2019, marks twenty-nine years since God miraculously saved me. I am alive! After the birth of my fifth child Kolya, the disease manifested itself again for the second time. But as you see, I am healthy now, and after all that happened to me, I gave birth to six more children.

My husband and I prayed every day since the day God healed me in America. I prayed for one hour in the morning, and we had prayer meetings in our house in the evenings. Until now, nothing has changed; I wait for everyone to come from work and I pray, asking the Lord to bless their way and the atmosphere in my family, not forgetting to pray for each one of my children.

Why did all this happen, and how did we understand the importance of prayer? I was never interested in how other people are praying. I only remember that when I was severely sick, my husband took me from the hospital to stay with my parents and my children for a few days. I heard how my father and mother were asking the Lord for my healing at night. Their prayers became another revelation about communication with our heavenly Father and support at those difficult times.

I had a good life. It was filled with God's mercy and miracles, and I can share some of them with you.

I don't remember exactly how old I was, but I recall the following incident. One day I returned late from the meeting. I lay down but was not able to sleep, so I started to pray and intercede, and wasn't able to stop. An hour passed, then another one, and I didn't understand what this prayer was about. What was happening?

Suddenly my son called me. He was supposed to come with his friends to spend the night with us that evening, and in the morning they were planning to climb up a mountain.

He called me at two in the morning and said, "Mom, we are not coming today. We will come tomorrow." I slept peacefully after talking to my son.

I saw the following picture when I woke up in the morning and came out of the house. My son and his friends were pulling a packed-up car. It turned out that they pulled up the car in front of a road ditch at night. There were five people in the car. I don't even want to imagine that all of them could have crashed if they hadn't pulled up the car on time. If it wasn't for the prayer, I don't know what might have happened!

Another evening, Valera, a young man of about seventeen or eighteen years old, came to our house and said that he was in a hurry and popped in for a minute. Young people were gathering together, and he was hurrying to join them. I told Petya that something smelled like a dead man before Valera came. When we decided to pray, Valera popped in. I offered him to join the prayer, but he refused because he was in a hurry. He left, but Petya and I continued to pray. I was getting ready to go to the morning meeting when not far from our house saw a smashed car. I rushed to find out what happened, and it turned out that Valera fell asleep at the wheel and crashed into a tree. Praise God, he was alive!

SISTERS

When my son Moses was twenty-four years old, I had a bad dream about him. It was as if the doctors were telling me that he was dead. I woke up abruptly from the dream and started to pray. It was 6:30 in the morning. I woke my husband up, and we started praying together, and the next day, I fasted and continued to pray for my son. Moses came to our house during lunch and told us the following story. He had loaded his car with 1.5 tons of parquets, and while driving, he slammed on the breaks sharply, and the load that was in the car flew into the driver's cabin, and it could have killed him in an instant, but he stayed alive. Oh, how God protects us!

One day in my dream, I saw an infant in a coffin. I was a grown-up woman already, so I went to my daughter-in-law's bedroom. They lived in our house with Valera. I told her about the vision, and we started to pray. While praying as a family, we were destroying the looming trouble and asked for God's protection. A few days later, my grandchildren were running around a huge mirror that was not nailed to the wall. They climbed up on the mirror, and it fell down. If at least one child had stayed next to the mirror, he would have died immediately. God protected our grandchildren!

Once, an infant died in our house. He was dead for a few minutes. We all started to pray, and Anya (the infant's mother) was crying out to the Lord in such a way that He brought him back to life.

Of course, having a large family demands hard work. I lie down to sleep, usually at one in the morning, but when I don't feel like sleeping, I read the Bible. I'll read two or three chapters, and when I become sleepy, I lie down to sleep.

The more I pray, the more I see God's miracles. Awake or asleep, God speaks to me, warning of danger and prompting me to pray.

My children love to pray, and it has already been nine years since we gathered together for a united prayer every Thursday. There were fifty-four people at prayer last time. While watching my children and grandchildren and recalling how I brought them up, I thought, *Nothing would have worked out without prayer. What would have happened to them all?* I truly don't know.

We wake up at seven in the morning. I turn on the Christian radio channel at 7:10, and join the prayer of Portland. After that I get ready for work and leave the house.

It has already been twenty-six years since I started working in America. For nine out of those years, I arranged weddings and many younger couples used my services. We were taught at an early age to maintain purity in our relationships, but now I notice that young people do not particularly care about this. Later on, they encounter great difficulties in return for their sinful lifestyles.

I can't say for sure if everything depends on a woman, but I can say that she has to bear everything and pray constantly.

My husband is a hard-working person. He works the whole day, and needs to rest when he comes home. I wait for the others to come home before I start praying. How can Petya stay awake until one o'clock in the morning to pray when he needs to get up at seven o'clock to go to work?

I always told my kids that their father is a hard worker and that it is good. I believe that is the reason they grew up as hard-working people too. We don't have lazy people in our family.

When children have a happy life, I believe it is because their mothers and fathers prayed for it. If a child's life is not arranged properly, then it's the parent's fault.

Our son Valera wasn't able to get married for a long time. He did a twenty-one day fast, stopped eating, was praying and waiting for an answer. After a while, God granted him a date with Anna. Now they have an amazing family and are bringing up their children.

I always told my children the following, "There are people who take their life seriously; they pray and bless their lives. Other people are so careless about God and family that they become unhappy with life."

Seven of our children are married. Some of them didn't meet their "one and only" at once. One of my daughters was engaged, but by God's grace, she didn't marry that man. She broke off the engagement because the groom was living in sin. At one point, one of our sons broke off his engagement too. I am happy that God protected them from unnecessary heartbreak.

My children who have their own families live blessed. I am so grateful to God for my five daughters-in-law. I am just as happy when I think about my sons-in-law. It's a genuine happiness to have a family that loves God.

Olga Alyokhina, Vera's Friend

I would like to tell you about Vera and how meeting her changed my life.

I was born and lived in Moscow. I am a musician; but beyond that, I love music with all my heart. For many years I studied and worked in this sphere. First, I graduated from a music school for gifted children, then university, and among my most favorite places were the Bolshoi Theater and the conservatoire.

When I married an American, I left my life enhanced with colors in Moscow and moved to America. The present turned out to be dull, and the past seemed so bright that I fell into depression.

Boredom became my constant friend, and I decided to go to church. I turned to faith, not because of the monotonous events that occurred in my life—I truly wanted to encounter the Lord and find the meaning of life; I had been to many churches searching for the living God, not just knowledge about Him. After two years, I knew many things about faith, but I never encountered God in person. Crying from powerlessness and loneliness, I prayed, and after a while received a word from one of the prophets that said the following, "Don't look for friends, I will send them to you Myself."

Two or three weeks had passed since that moment, and I ended up to be in the same place where my dear, but at that time, unfamiliar Vera was. She came up to me, and we started a nice conversation, after which she invited me to join a prayer meeting that was going to take place in her house.

When I saw her, it was as if something clicked inside me; it was like I had found my soul sister. I wanted to see her again! Unfortunately, we didn't see each other for two or three months. I was suffering from that because I felt that she was a special person in my life.

We met each other at one of the meetings after a while, and I literally caught hold of Vera and immediately exchanged phone numbers with her and asked for the address to the prayer meeting.

I found myself in a huge house where Vera brought me. We had a little conversation at the end of the meeting; I shared with her and her husband how good I felt by experiencing God's presence at their house. I found God in their house! They did not seem important-looking or businesslike to me at all; on the contrary, they behaved modestly, and their actions told me more about love than words could.

I realized that evening that at last, I was free to feel calm and natural, like a bird in a flight or a musician playing music. It was both something new and desirable for me! I was breathing freely as if I had wings, and nothing could stop me at that moment. I think that was the day I became a true believer in God.

Vera asked me if I lived far from them and suggested moving closer. I agreed without thinking twice. I was living in Beaverton at that time, but after some time I moved to a house next to Vera's place.

In church and during my fellowship with Vera, I felt peace and an extraordinary feeling that everything is in its place as it should be. While I had an education and I read and thought a lot about the structure of the world, I understood that it was the knowledge that prevented me from finding God. During these last years in America, I diligently sought Him because only prayer brough me peace.

One thing I like to watch is how Vera's husband is treating her and their relationship in their family. There's so much sincerity and love in it. No matter how gorgeous I looked whenever I came to their house, in spite of their modest appearance and attire, they never condemned me for the rings, jewelry, or the outfits that I wore, and even my manners were accepted calmly in their family.

It's true; I was used to my colorful life in Moscow. My house was seven minutes away from Kreml, and here in America, I attend different festivals and operas, and it never embarrassed them. These ordinary people loved me sincerely and accepted me into their home.

Vera's spirit is so close to mine. She is both my instructor and friend. So many times, I called her and told her that I am heading to Seattle, and she would answer without hesitation, "I'm coming with you."

Once I confused the flights and the day of departure to Italy. I was spending my time peacefully and without any rush at home, thinking that we were leaving tomorrow. Suddenly I received a call from my friend, saying, "Where are you? We need to be at the airport within half an hour." I was simultaneously packing my luggage and calling Vera, "Please, come! I am running late for my flight!" That was the fastest trip to the airport, and I think I was the last passenger on board.

My grandmother is an orthodox, and for as long as I can remember, she had always prayed for my salvation. All her life, she spent long hours on her knees, praying and reading the Bible in Old Slavonic. I think that mostly I was hiding away from God because I was told once that my family would be saved through me. I looked for alternatives all my life—just to get lost in them.

That's when I met Vera and found myself in their family. Oh, how they love God and treat everyone kindly. That was what I needed: sincerity—something that people do, but not to surprise others or to look sophisticated by using smart words. No!

Vera's prayers and her attitude toward me was essential for me. One day I came to their house, and I had caught a cold and had a slight temperature. Vera was simply sitting next to me and telling me something, and I felt so good. I was sitting on the sofa with her, and we started laughing so hard that the cold was gone. There wasn't a trace of the temperature or the malaise. Miracles!

Her prayers and friendship are not fake. They come from her heart, and that is the reason that it is so genuine.

MARIA KOZLOVA

M y mother is no lon- ger with us, but I will tell you about her with great pleasure. Maria Ilinichna Kozlova was born in 1926. She was from the Molokans, who were once exiled to Armenia and other regions of the South Caucasus. They say that the Molokans always outstand with their strong faith. Some of them trusted in God's Word, others trusted more in personal communication with God, but one way or another, they honored the Lord and refrained from all sinful things; you would never see them use drugs, alcohol, or cigarettes.

So my mother was stronger spiritually than physically. Long ago, my grandfather departed from the community of believers and became a Baptist, for which he was imprisoned, and my mother backed him up. He was baptized with the Holy Spirit in prison and started speaking in other tongues, as described in Acts. When my grandfather was released from prison, his family didn't accept him; neither the Molokans nor the Baptists were able to understand what was going on with him. However, through him, the movement of the Holy Spirit started in those regions. My mother was the first to understand that speaking in other tongues was the natural manifestation of the Spirit of God. For a long time, my father didn't believe in or didn't accept the revelation that my grandfather had. But since then, my mother was baptized in the Spirit, my father put up with it, and after a while, he started speaking in other tongues too.

Bold and strong, that's how I remember my mother. Only eleven children out of fourteen were born alive, and those eleven children were brought up in love and respect.

How did my parents feed the family? We had a cow, so we never ran out of dairy products in our house. Curds, milk, butter, and cheese; even if there was no other food to eat, you would never go hungry with these dairy products.

Despite the fact that we had a large family, we hosted many guests in our home. I don't recall a single moment when we were all by ourselves in our house. Even if our parents were not at home, we knew perfectly well about the treasured cooking pot envisioned for the guests. We didn't have a telephone at home, and my mother and father quite often paid visits to the sick or the believers. And instead of our parents, when people knocked at our door, we would open the door and receive the guests.

In the cooking pot, there was usually either potatoes or a freshly made borsh. Our parents didn't allow us to eat from the cooking pot; they were thinking of the guests.

Our village was located next to the junction station, and some people came to our house to wait for the next train.

There was an elderly man who would walk three kilometers from the train station to our house just to spend at least an hour studying the word of God with my father. My father knew the exact time of this man's arrival, and he was waiting for him. Usually, that man entered the house with the following words, "Brother, I have an hour until my next train arrives, so let's pray." So, they spent time in prayer and fellowship. My mother would lay the table, and after an hour, the man would take his bag, hang it over his shoulder and go to the station.

Our family's hospitality was expressed though feeding and sheltering people. My mother and father were not the only ones who took care of us and the guests; everyone in the house had responsibilities. While we grew up, the responsibilities changed, but one thing remained—the evening prayer and taking care of the guests.

My responsibility was to make crepes once or twice a week. Crepes are an inexpensive dish, but they are very nourishing: it's delicious both with sour cream or jam and with meat filling or cottage cheese! I made no less than 150 crepes at a time. The next day, guests would eat all the crepes that I made. Usually, the children gave up their beds to the guests, and slept either on the chest or the sofa. In the most extreme cases, we slept on the floor where my mother made a place for us to sleep.

We lived in prosperity; at home, we had two washing machines with hand-wringers. In winter, ropes were stretched inside the house, and we hung the linen, sheets, and clothes on them. Dry bed sheets were replaced with freshly washed ones. That was a non-stop, endless cycle. Of course, I was told that my mother used to boil the linen in an iron wash pot before; this process was not only a long one but a difficult one as well. But after a while, my father was able to find washing machines, and it eased my mother's load. In old photos, you could often see my mother doing laundry.

My siblings and me grew up in this environment. Our parents are generous people, but at the same time, they taught us how to handle money carefully, in other words, to live within our means. They would say, "If you have ten rubles for today and you spend twelve, then tomorrow you will have eight rubles at your disposal. But do not take more so as not to create debts. You'd rather share what you have than accumulate debts."

My mother and father taught us to help people when they were in need. They were our role models in everything they taught us to do. We were already living in a new house in 70s, and although it was not big, we always had one spare room for the guests.

In summer, the flow of guests to our house never stopped. Young people often came to our neighborhood from villages and spent the night in our house. My father redid the barns next to the main building into bedrooms; it was great to stay there in the summer! You could hear songs being played with a guitar or accordion every evening in our house. Some of the newcomers were baptized with the Holy Spirit, for others, we prayed, or simply read the Bible together, more having fellowship about spiritual things. I grew up with these conversations, my faith strengthened, and at one point, I realized that God was all I needed in this life.

SISTERS

At one point, I was so carried away by the world that it seemed I was leading a double life unnoticed by others. I learned how to close the door quietly behind me so that no one heard how I sneaked home late at night. However, I understood that it would upset my parents when they found out everything.

One evening, I closed the front door behind me with a habitual movement, but when I reached the room where my parents were sitting, I eavesdropped on their prayer:

"Lord, maybe we were mistaken in something, please forgive us and reveal it to us, or maybe we became the reason for temptation for our son. Help us to be the example that will draw our child closer to You."

I stood there and thought that it was not their fault that I was so infatuated by the world; it was my choice. But it was so unpleasant for me knowing that I had caused them to feel that pain. The simple prayer of my parents touched my heart. After that day, I was not able to regain my peace; I was so ashamed. After a while, I repented wholeheartedly and tried to keep myself in purity.

There were also governmental officials who came to our house. They usually came to write down the names of the people who gathered at our house. Sometimes they would confiscate the Christian literature, or they would issue a fine after searching the house.

My mother would gather the children and teach the following after we had this type of "guest":

"You know, children, it's a great honor to be persecuted for the sake of Jesus Christ. We don't have to be sad but happy because we are lucky enough to pass through our portion of suffering today. And although they took something that was very dear to us, God will bless us through this. It's written in His Word that it's a great honor to be persecuted for His sake."

Mom tried to bring examples from the Bible, where the disciples of Christ sang and prayed while they were being imprisoned.

You didn't want to complain about the government or the circumstances after such words. We considered those inspections as an honor.

Yes, you could call our house a small church. And the fact that it stayed the way it was when we grew up is mainly due to my mother. Her sincere love for God set an example for a relationship with the Lord and us. There was not a shadow of slyness in my mother. She was always honest and open, and she did not impose prayer or spiritual requirements on us.

Mom didn't preach; rather she told people about her life. About how God led her and what temptations she had to overcome. My mother and father not only shared stories of their victories with us, but sometimes they told us stories about the times when they faced difficulties and how they withstood them and fought against temptations. Consequently, it helped me to walk through my personal temptations.

95

SISTERS

Of course, in our house, it was accepted to read the Word of God and pray either together or separately. When we were little, my mother read the Bible to us and the stories that she had written about Christians. My mother had many journals where you could find stories about such people as Pavel Smolny, the stories of the persecution of Christians, stories about the deportation of the believers to Armenia, the Tsarist-era, and how the Molokans survived during the times of Nicholay II. It was a hard time for our nation. They had to hide in caves and live in huts.

My mother read stories and told us about the faithfulness of Christians in those hard times. Sometimes she started telling the first part of the story, and we impatiently had to wait until the next day to listen to the second part of it.

We enjoyed preparing for family holidays even more than talking with my mother in the evenings. All the children helped to roll out the dough and make sweets and pies, while some adults recalled a story from either their or other Christian's lives. And all of us attentively listened to the lazy talk that was going on in between them. The younger ones asked questions, the older sisters added what they remembered, and this united us so much that everyone felt so good and warm to be at home.

Despite the fact that she never forced us to pray, my mother's morning prayers were the best example of the fellowship with God for me.

But it's funny to remember with what thrill we looked forward to the evening prayer. My mother usually told us a story or read something from Scripture, then would ask one of us to start praying. Sophisticated words were out of the question while praying; prayer had always been something sincere, coming from the heart. And if mom said, "Sergey, pray!" and he was silent, then she knew that something was wrong in his heart.

So all the children got ready for the evening prayer, waiting for their turn to pray. My mother wanted to make prayer a personal thing for us, so we would present to the Lord our personal thoughts and requests rather than pray according to a formula or pre-set standard. Despite age, each of the children looked inside their own hearts, checking whether God was living there or not and what they would like to say to the Creator.

If one of the children understood that his heart was full of offense, they would go either to mom or dad to confess it to them during the day. We were not sure that we would wake up to see a new day, and we didn't want to stand in front of God as sinners.

This was the norm in our family. Our parents taught us to keep our hearts and be sincere with God.

Let me tell about my father.

He was a stove-maker by his profession. He worked a lot, and when his main job was over, he earned extra money on the side. Dad was also appointed as a minister over several regions near us, so sometimes he took his motorcycle, one of the children, or the ministers and set out to help people. Sometimes he was absent for several days, and all the responsibilities of the house fell on my mother's shoulders.

My mother was never upset about this. She simply said, "Dad is set over us by God, and everything he does is for the Lord. This means that God will find ways for taking care of his family."

My father was very attentive to us when he was at home. I remember quite well that he used to lie down on the floor and allow the little ones to climb up over him. When we grew up, we were walking over his back doing some sort of a massage. But when we became more mature, we talked with my father about different topics. Although that time didn't last long, it was the most precious moments ever.

When we needed to be disciplied, my mother interpreted the punishment this way, "God set your father in charge over the whole family, and if someone does something wrong then its solely the father's right to show him the right way."

Frankly, my father was very kind. After apologizing to him for our wrongdoings, we could avoid the punishment the first time. But if we committed the same mistake twice we understood quite well that we wouldn't be able to avoid the punishment. Mom always added, "Should the father, who takes care of us and works from morning till evening, have to be upset with you or punish you? He thinks about how to feed and clothe you, and then when he comes home, he wants peace and serenity. So why should he scold you for your bad behavior?"

That was quite fair. Most of us tried not to upset my father over trifles. We felt it in our hearts; why do bad things and upset our beloved ones?

My grandmother was a true miracle. She had seventy grandchildren and she knew them all by name; she never asked their names twice. It's interesting that all of her grandchildren respected and visited this nice friend of theirs until her last breath.

Her grandchildren turned to her for a piece of advice when it came down to dating. Grandmother always expressed her opinion about the person, and if he was kind and worthy in her eyes, then she usually said the following, "I will pray for both of you so that everything turns out well."

My grandma's house was always filled with people. My mother and I wanted my grandmother to stay with us during her last days of life, but she brushed off our offer, saying, "My house is the place where all of you meet. That's what I wanted. I am not alone."

Yes, she was exactly like that. My grandmother could joke in such a way that she made everyone laugh hard. And she loved to express her opinion straightforwardly but with love, and we always listened to her advice. My grandmother always gave an explanation for what she liked and disliked.

The most outstanding example of someone who led godly life was my mom. I especially remember how sensitive she was toward God and how sincere and simple she was in communicating with Him and people.

My mother often gave answers to our questions after prayer led by the Holy Spirit. As kids, we ran to her to tell her our problems and ask for advice. My mother prayed for us, and God gave her wisdom, not only to give us advice, but also to speak things into our hearts that were only known to God.

My mother loved going to the garden quite often to stay alone and pray. There was always someone in the house, and oftentimes there was not enough room for having peaceful fellowship with the Lord. That was why she would either go to the barn or to the garden. Her favorite place was the bench under the cherry tree, and there, away from all of us, she poured her heart out to the Lord.

She entered the house a totally new person after her time in prayer. Sometimes she had clear answers to our situations or a revelation for the whole family.

She was a wonderful woman. And as an inheritance, she left 11 children, 70 grandchildren, 165 great-grandchildren, and 26 great-great-grandchildren who were lucky to see her while she was alive. Now there are even more in number to our family.

VALENTINA AGAPOVA

Told by Valentina's son Vladimir

Valentina Ivanovna Aga-
pova, that's what my
mother was called. She is with
God now, but I will tell you a
little bit about her life. People
who knew my mother often
repeated that a monument
should be erected in her honor.
She was a saint for many people. She is remembered in our
family as the keeper of peace.

My mother was born in Orenburg. She was four or five
years old when she left her birthplace and moved to Ukraine
with my grandmother. Her father was a drunkard. Her mother
was afraid of him. So when he left to the front, she packed
her belongings and left.

They moved to Kazakhstan, where neither her father nor her relatives could find them. My mother never saw her father again, but she knew that he was looking for them.

My mother became a believer when she was older. She met her future husband and they both became Christians, got married, and moved to live in Uzbekistan. The church usually gathered at homes. Sometimes people gathered at our house, but the location for meetings was changed quite often. The gatherings occurred secretly, concealed both from the government and the society.

***

Nikolay Agapov, Valentina's Husband

I married Valya in 1957. I saw her for the first time at our neighbor's wedding, who lived across the road. I often played accordion or chromatic accordion at that time, so people invited me as a musician to play for their events. Most of my friends were there, and I knew almost all of them, but I saw one of the girls for the first time. And that was where I noticed her. I kept looking sideways to where she was sitting while I playing the accordion and was photographing young people. The wedding was in full swing, but Valentina was getting ready to go home. When she was ready to leave, I left my accordion and followed her.

"Hey, can I speak to you for a minute?"

"What you want from me?"

"Please, stand over here," I asked her while grabbing my camera.

"But why?" she didn't concede.

"You'll know later."

The girl stood straight, and I took a picture of her. I was lucky to see her off before she went home that day. It became the day of our acquaintance and first date.

***

Mom and dad had nine children, and I was one of the youngest. They brought us up in difficult times. Dad made good money, but it was still not enough, so mom had to work even while she was pregnant.

My mother would take her eldest child to kindergarten on her way to the textile factory, and then she went to work afterward. I don't think it was easy for her, however, who cared if it was easy or not? She had to work to feed the newborns. And God took care of me while I was in my mother's womb.

By the time my younger brother and I were born, my mother no longer worked at the factory. She looked after the children, but she still helped my father by earning extra money on the side however she could. It was good that I and my brother didn't have to go to kindergarten. I was happy to stay home, surrounded by my family. The eldest children took care of the younger ones while our parents were working.

Starting from the age of four, I remember our life quite clearly and what my mother and father were busy with. From that day on, everything turned out good.

We moved to a new house. Before my father became a bee-keeper, my mother, who was breastfeeding a child, sometimes had to starve for three days because she gave everything to her children, then since that moment our family began to live satisfyingly. Now, dad had his personal business, and he worked hard. We had bees, and we helped my father to take care of them. My father also worked as a photographer, so my mother colored in the portraits, retouched them, and removed the flaws from people's faces.

My mother had to take public service work because the state had its own way of defining the duties of its citizens. In addition to everything that she was already doing, imagine that she had to clean the institute and sweep the streets. Of course, we were helping her with that. In addition, our whole family would growing flowers, and my mother sold them in the bazaar. Labor really unites people, and it was manifested in our family in the best possible way. Everyone helped each other; we did everything together, both around the house and outside of it.

Our parents made sure that we were taken care of first. I remember that my mother always cut the chicken and gave the best part, the drumstick, to my father, then she gave a huge piece of meat to each of the children, and she would eat the liver or the feet—parts that the rest of the family wouldn't eat. This simple example of love toward her beloved ones left a great impact on me.

Honestly, I don't remember how I became a Christian. I think it's because I was a Christian since my birth. I "learned at mother's knee."

Parental example served as a bridge to reach out to God. Our faith was strengthened by their works, love, and dedication day by day. My mother's sacrificial nature and the desire to live in peace and harmony amazed me. When my brothers and sister were fighting, she tried to smooth out the conflicts by reconciling them rather than judging.

Mom's respect for my father was endless, and she obeyed him in everything. For today's young girls, her behavior may seem strange, but it was quite natural for her. She neither criticized or backtalked him. Everybody said the same thing about her, "She is holy, and a monument should be erected to her." I have never heard people saying those things about other people that I know.

She was respected by the Christians of various denominations because my mother didn't really care to which denomination a person belonged to. If somebody simply needed help or her smile, she eagerly shared with them whatever she had at that moment. My mother treated everyone equally well. She loved the church, especially singing there.

My father was a strict person. If we did something wrong, we knew that we wouldn't be able to avoid dad's punishment. We knew that in the evening, dad was going to punish us for sure, and it felt like stormy clouds accumulating over our house. That was why when dad came home, if we had done something wrong, while we opened the gates to let him in we tried to stay out of sight, hoping that a miracle would happen and we would avoid punishment.

Sometimes dad asked us to show him our report cards. He rarely checked our report cards, every once in six months, but I remember those moments very well because my father gave me such a blow on my bottom those days! The price for our behavior was as follows; if you received a D, you got one blow with a belt on your bottom, if it was an F or bad behavior (my teacher would grade me with an F when she was very angry with me), then you received two blows with the belt on your bottom.

Interestingly, after the punishment, I had enough consciousness to study as much as I felt pain. Then everything started anew, except I tried to avoid getting into dad's sight. And if it was time for report cards, I tried to avoid him for a couple of days.

I never paid enough attention to my studies at school. I thought of becoming either a photographer or a beekeeper or all of them together. The most important thing was that my future had already been predestined and didn't depend on knowledge.

My grades were so bad in the fifth grade that at the beginning of the last quarter, my parents were called to the school to speak not only to one teacher, but all of them at once. My grades and behavior weren't good at all. My mother came to school because dad was not at home; he was on a vacation in Ukraine. I still remember that day as if it was yesterday. I was so ashamed! My mother went from one teacher to another, listening to what a bad student her son was. The class teacher accompanied her, showing my grades and complaining about my abominable behavior. My mother was crying. I felt very sorry for her, but how could I comfort her when what the teachers said was true?

In the evening, without saying any word about what she heard and learned at school, my mother served me dinner.

That day my conscience woke up; how could I grieve her so? The last quarter I finished with Bs and As, and I even participated in the scholastic competition in biology.

It was neither the fear from my parents nor punishment that influenced my studies and career choice. My mother's kindness gave me a space to think and to change for the better. Until now,

SISTERS

I still believe that we need to influence people with kindness, not with fear.

I deserved punishment, and was waiting for it to happen when my father came back from his vacation. But my mother said nothing to him. She had forgiven me, and it seemed that she had forgotten the shame that she went through because of me. I remembered that lesson my mother taught me throughout my whole life and tried to apply it in the lives of my children too.

I noticed that for her, there was no distinction between someone who treated her well and someone who hurt or offended her family. She knew how to forgive. One of my sisters divorced her husband, and later I learned that my mother was in touch with him. He used to come to her house, and they talked. By the way, she kept peace with all of her daughters-in-law and sons-in-law. It was her service to be in peace with everyone.

VALENTINA AGAPOVA

As you probably understand, our family was open to receive other people. My father and mother would have guests quite often, sometimes even unexpected ones. People came to our house from different places. They knocked at our door with the following words, "We know you are believers. Can we stay at your house?"

Of course, my parents invited them into the house and fit all of them in however they could. We were little children, but we gave up our beds to the guests with great pleasure and slept on the couches.

One day there were tirty-three people in our house, and we found a place for all of them to sleep. They had come to the city for a wedding. They were mainly young people, and our house was so noisy and filled with joy those days. It was interesting to observe and communicate with them together with my brothers and sisters. And my mother was tirelessly busy around the house. It's interesting, but I don't remember her complaining or murmuring at the guests. She always cooked and cleaned the house with great pleasure and a good mood.

I remember quite well that since I was six years old, my mother would send me the nearest bakery to buy bread. I would buy ten loaves of bread for each day. When we were having guests, I had to run for bread several times a day, and the baker was surprised. He wanted to know why I was buying so much bread. I was answering him happily, "We have a large family and we have guests today." Then I would run home with the warm loaves of bread.

SISTERS

I recall more good memories from my family's life, but there's one sad story. My mother was standing in a line to buy potatoes, and when her turn came, the crowd from behind started to boil over. Why? My mother bought a little bit more than the others, and they were worried that there wouldn't be enough potatos for everyone.

As if apologizing, she said that she had nine children at home to feed.

To which she received a sarcastic reply, "We know people like you! You had fun with men, gave birth to children, and now you have to feed that crowd of hungry mouths."

My mother apologetically repeated, "I gave birth to my children when I was married. I have only one husband."

She went home, taking the potatoes she bought under the condemning glances of the people in line. She cried bitterly after this incident. No, my mother did not hold any grudge against people, but you must admit that they accused her unfairly. If they only knew back then that she had received an "Order of Parental Glory" for having a large family and that she had a miscarriage and mourned the loss of her child. However, in spite of everything, her characteristic trait was to forgive from the bottom of her heart, and in my adulthood, she taught me many times how should I act in different situations.

And when she died, it was hard for me to accept that I wouldn't be able to see her anymore. My sister didn't tell me that mom died; she told me that mom was taken to the hospital. She didn't have the courage to tell me the truth.

A few months before her death my mother told me not to worry about her. "I know where I'm going. Don't worry that much," she said.

"Mom, don't speak like that. Please, live a little bit more," I begged her like a child.

I was always afraid to lose her. When I was a child and my mother fell sick, I prayed fervently for her not to die. And as an adult, I anxiously watched every ambulance that passed through our area.

I had a hard time putting up with my mother's absence. Ten years have passed, but I still remember the meetings and conversations we had with her.

I borrowed a small but very cool bus from a friend for a week to take my family to Florida shortly before her death. We decided to take my mother with us because she dreamed of being there.

During the trip, she was fascinated by everything that surrounded her. "Look, just look around; beauty is everywhere! Can you imagine what a wonderful dwelling God has prepared for us?"

I replied calmly, "Mom, please don't talk now about what awaits us with God. I still want to see you around us. It's too early to think about heaven."

A week after we returned home, I was so busy during the week that I didn't find the time to go see my mother, not even once. One evening, my wife told me to go to her house with instructions to either take or bring the vacuum cleaner. I remember our conversation with her, "Mom, why do you look so tired? Are you sick?"

"Is it apparent?"

"Yes."

"It's hard to breathe; maybe it's asthma again," my mother answered silently.

She had flowers all over the house, and she was also growing tulips. Asthma could have been intensified because of the blooming season. But I was not familiar with heart and allergic diseases, that was why I was surprised at my own question, "Mom, what if something is wrong with your heart?"

"No, no, it's impossible."

"Mom, please go to the doctor."

"Yes, I will go tomorrow."

"And what if you won't manage to?"

"I will. Don't worry," she simply answered.

I kissed her goodbye and looked straight into her eyes to keep in mind the color of her eyes and how she looked. I think it was the first time that I really looked at my mother like that. I thought to myself, *Lord, let our meeting be not the last one.* And I left.

A few days later, I was waiting for my friend Lyova next to his house. I opened the newspaper while sitting inside my car and saw a note about someone's funeral. Four of the relatives of this person were standing next to the coffin at the grave in the picture next to the text. I thought that there would be more people at my mother's funeral. I remembered my grandmother as well. She was seventy-four when she died, and my mother was seventy-one at that time.

"Lord, please prolong my mother's life and give her a chance to live until seventy-four." But honestly, even that was not enough for me; I wanted her to live longer.

Dad recalls the last days with my mother in his own way. They reveal both my mother's character and the relationship of two loving people.

***

In the evening, we went to bed early, and Valya told me, "I will die soon, but you will live longer than me."

"You'll manage to bury more than one person like me!" I got angry at her words.

"No!" Valya didn't understand jokes, and that was why she answered me abruptly. "You are my first and the last one."

"Valya, what's bothering you? Everything is ok, right? Your heart is fine; you don't have diabetes or problems with your stomach."

"Yes, only my feet are not okay. If they were only able to replace them, then they would serve me hundred more years for sure," she said, and we laughed.

"That's why darling, you will live longer than me. I will die first," I insisted.

"No, I will die first, and you will get married again."

"Sorry, but you are mistaken! I am seventy-two, and even if you die earlier than me, what do you think? Will I be able to live with someone else but you?"

"Will you carve in the headstone the following: "My path has passed through beautiful places, and my heritage is pleasant for me?" I felt a lump in my throat when I heard these words and wasn't able to object to anything else.

We slept a little and talked for a long time that night. In the morning, Valya asked me to take her to the doctor. While combing her hair, she continued the conversation we had started the night before.

"I have a sin," Valya said and fell silent.

My eyes nearly popped out of my head, and I didn't know what to say. Was it possible that she hid something from me or lied to me? No, it couldn't be.

"Jealousy is my sin."

"Oh, c'mon, you scared me to death!" I answered. "Who is not jealous these days? Most probably the ones who don't know what love is. I don't believe that you can love someone without being jealous of them."

Valya fell silent as she finished combing her hair, and we went to the doctor. On our way to the doctor, she recalled something and started speaking actively.

"Kolya, you are writing, aren't you? Continue to write. Don't stop."

"But you were insisting that I should leave writing and go fishing!" I objected, surprised.

"No! Continue to write," she answered silently.

"I have bad handwriting and don't like the way I write."

"I would have never told you, but I have read your writings."

"When did you manage to read my notes?" I was surprised again.

"You write, and then you leave your notes on the table, don't you? That's when I read them."

"Okay." That was the only answer that I could give to her.

While Valya was getting out of the car, a thought came to my mind. "Valya!" I called out for my wife.

"What's wrong?"

"Come back."

SISTERS

Valya came up to the car and asked, "So, what's wrong?"

"You say that you will die soon. But all I see is you flourishing day by day, just like me," I answered her, smiling.

"Where do you know it from?" she smiled back at me.

"There's no other way! Where's your cane?"

Valya smiled and went around the car to get her cane. Of course, she didn't walk with a cane constantly, but this time she decided to take it with her and walked to the entrance of the hospital smiling.

Usually while I was waiting for my wife, I would fall asleep in the car, but this time I was not able to take a nap because of two ambulances, which drove up to the hospital one after another. The hospital porters carried away the stretcher, and I went inside the building as well.

"Where is Valentina?" I asked the nurse.

"She is here," the girl pointed in an indefinite direction.

I decided to go to the doctor's consulting room, but the police officer didn't allow me to enter. Then I understood everything immediately. Then they carried out Valya on the stretcher, and she was covered in wires. I wanted to go with her in the ambulance car, but everyone pushed me away from it, so I quickly ran back to my car. The hospital porters explained to me that I could go in the driver's cab.

We arrived at the hospital, and my wife was attached to some devices, which the nurses kept turning on and off. They had called my daughter, Nadya, and we sat next to each other, not understanding anything that was happening.

One of the doctors came to my daughter and whispered something in English into her ear. Nadya cried silently.

"Is she dead?" I asked.

"Yes, Dad, she is," answered Nadya.

I never got married again. There will be none like my Valentina, neither in heaven nor on the earth. She was more than a hero for me. My incredible one.

***

My mother went to be with the Lord while in the hospital, and I didn't know about it. While I was waiting for my friend and getting ready to take the children from school, I answered my sister's phone call. She said, "Come to the hospital, Mom had a heart attack." I went there immediately, praying to myself that everything was okay with mom, but unfortunately by that time she was dead.

I learned later that she went to the doctor's appointment dressed beautifully, as she usually liked to do. Despite the fact that she wasn't feeling good, she took care of herself in the best possible way and chose the clothes she wanted to wear.

The doctor checked her heart and didn't find any defects in it, but nevertheless, sent her to pass an examination. My mother didn't refuse; she only smiled at him. The doctor smiled back while filling out her medical card. After a few seconds, the doctor looked at her and noticed that her head was hanging over her shoulder. She went to be with the Lord quietly and in an instant.

At my mother's funeral, the church was full, and not everyone was able to get inside. Not only did parishioners came to the funeral to honor the memory of my mother, but the mayor of the city, as well as teachers from our college where we studied English. I can't name them all. People were drawn to her all her life, not because she preached fervently or was popular but because my mother loved the people who surrounded her and treated everyone with sincere kindness.

I regret that I wasn't able to spend a little bit more time with her, to breathe in her warmth and have a heart-to-heart talk one more time. Ten years later, I still miss her so much.

ANNA TRACHUK

That day, I woke up early in the morning and left for Portland. I stopped by a café where my friend Ivan Trachuk was waiting for me. Vanya is a pastor in Portland, and we have known each other for a long time. We were talking about things that were very dear to us during breakfast; we were talking about God, the Bible, and the church. Then involuntarily, we started talking about his mom.

— Artur Simonyan

My mother, Anna Trachuk, gave birth to six sons and two daughters. We all grew up as Christians, and six of us became ministers at church.

As far as I remember, according to what my mother told us, she became a believer when she was little. When she became a Christian, she asked God for a husband who would serve Jesus, preach the Word of God, and prove himself as a man of God in practice. That was my mother's dream. During her wedding, she prayed like this,

"God, if he is not going to serve You and believe in You with his whole heart, then let this wedding be canceled."

They married, and later, my father became a minister just like my mother. We were born a little later.

My mother was very close to me. She was next to us day and night. She repeated one phrase every day without ceasing: "You will grow up and serve the Lord." Despite the political system in the country, and I am sure you remember, too, that communism did not encourage faith in Christ, my mother blessed us every morning and told us that we would preach the gospel to other people. Where did she get such faith from? I think she didn't pay attention to the circumstances but lived by the words she declared into her life.

Well, I didn't doubt my calling for too long. I became a pastor because since my childhood, I knew who I would be.

Mom paid attention to each child in the family, even though there were many of us. She found time to have personal fellowship with each one of us.

Of course, I can be called her favorite child, because my parents prayed for me a lot because I wasn't supposed to be born. In the beginning, her pregnancy was going well, but at some point, my mother turned to a doctor because she had complaints. At the hospital, she was told that the fetus wasn't moving or growing. "We have to do an abortion." this was their final verdict. But my mother didn't agree to an abortion, and she carried me against the doctor's instructions. She prayed without ceasing until I started moving in her womb.

Her prayer was much like the prayer of Hannah, who was barren and prayed in the temple to the Lord, saying, "Lord, I give this child to you, he doesn't belong to me, he is Yours." After a year, she gave birth to her son Samuel. I was a true miracle from heaven for my parents. This incident became known not only to our family but also to the doctors from that hospital and to our relatives.

Because of the miracle of my birth, I had great faith in Jesus, even as a child. Sometimes this was not met with kindness. Did I consider myself a black sheep at school or in any other place? Yes, maybe. But honestly, I liked it. I loved to defend my principles, to stand in front of the whole class, and say that I believe in God; I read the Bible and go to church. It was not difficult for me. I considered it an advantage and not something to be ashamed of. I think this confidence in God was instilled in me by my mother. She believed in Jesus with her whole heart and taught us to do the same.

I remember that our house was not far from the church. So everyone who came to the church meetings from other countries or villages stayed with us. Our house played the role of some kind of a unique "corridor." People stayed at our house, had dinner with us, and later, all of us would either go to the prayer meeting or stay in our house to worship God.

Sometimes our guests were eating food that we had never eaten. All the best was saved for the guests. We didn't receive any financial support from the church for feeding or hosting the guests in our house. My mother and father were just very hospitable people. It was seldom possible to guess exactly how many people there would be or whether we had ready-made food in the house, but my mother always had something in store for such occasions. A large casserole of borsh, which could be eaten for two or three days, saved the day more than once.

Whenever we had guests, we let them sleep in our beds, and we slept in the attic. We had hay there sometimes, and we slept so well on it. Sometimes we came up with some simple ideas instead of beds. but it never bothered us because it was so good to have guests in our home! The adults were having fellowship, and with great joy, we would listen to their stories about God and the persecution of Christians. The guests usually spoke about the conditions that the believers had to live in, about the persecution of Christians, about who had already been imprisoned who had become believers. The conversations lasted until morning, and they were so interesting to me!

Now our family has friends all over the world; those who once ate fried potatoes with us, or drank tea with the pies made by my mother, and went to the church meeting with us the next day.

In those days, outside our house was the Soviet Union, but inside the house was God's kingdom. Two different worlds existed so close to each other, but I liked the world where God and my family were the most. I have never imagined myself outside the church—never even dreamed of something unrelated to the ministry. My thoughts about the future were mainly composed of service and life in communion with God.

Of course, everything was because of my mother. She secretly brought Christian books for us from abroad. And one of the first of those books was "The King from the House of David." I usually read and re-read the book at night, because during the day, my brothers and sisters were reading it. Once my mother was detained at the border under the article of "smuggling" such literature into the country, but she was not sent to prison. She already had an Order of Parental Glory at that time, and thanks to having a large family, she was not imprisoned.

You might be wondering what theological education our parents and us had gotten. We all received a Christian education at home, and none of us studied in a Bible school or seminary. Miracles happened during prayer because we prayed not just for the sake of praying but with faith in the living God. Prophecies proclaimed in our house were being fulfilled after a while. There was a great expectation that stadiums, community buildings, and other public places would open their doors to preach the gospel to people.

I'm not sure how relationships were formulated in other Christian families because I knew that there were difficulties in my friends' families. The Lord was so real to every child in our family, and our parents were so dedicated to Him that they became such a great example for us of the grace of God that we did not want to abandon our faith or live differently. We grew up with the Lord, and we serve in the house of God to this day.

I often heard the following proverb in my family, "The devil finds work for idle hands to do." Well, well, our parents kept us busy before anyone else could. Not only my father, who always returned home late in the evening, had to work in order to feed a large family, but all of us worked hard. I don't remember any of the children being idle; all of them had something to do according to their strength.

We took care of our vegetable garden, and grew potatoes and other vegetables there. Each of the children took turns in helping mom in the kitchen—try feeding a family of ten with only bread and vegetables!

All of us dreamed of wearing good clothes, that was why our parents bought rabbits and a cow. We took good care of them and sold them for meat by the fall. Then the whole family were dressed well with the money earned from selling the meat. I think that our clothes were better than the clothes of the others; and our parents did their best to bless the families we knew however they could.

Honestly, if you ask me now whether my parents had time to communicate with one another, the only option that comes up to my mind is family prayer time. My father came home from work in the evening, and after work, he would go serve others. He would take us with him, and it was a great joy to go on a journey like that! At the age of eight or nine, I prayed for people by laying my hands on them. So we traveled to villages, served with my father, and my mother blessed our work. That's the whole romance.

I don't remember a single day when my mother asked my dad to stay home with her. With parting words and prayer, she saw us off to service. Sometimes we fasted together as a whole family because we had to pray over severely sick and possessed people the next day.

My mother taught us to respect our parents and God, and be kind toward people. The parishes were small, with 200-300 people in each. And quite often, the problems and questions that referred to church were discussed in our house. I can't say that there was condemnation in their conversations. Together, they tried to solve the problems and meet the needs of the believers and the parish.

SISTERS

Until now, I remember my mother's instructions that inspired me since my childhood. As it's written in the Proverbs, "Listen, my son, to your father's instruction and do not forsake your mother's teaching," my mother taught me as well.

My mother asked me to be careful with girls and marry someone who would have the same thoughts and goals as me, in other words, to make a lifetime choice. She spoke to my heart as if she knew my secret desires and hopes. I clearly remember her words, "Hold on to God and love Him with all your heart. Even if you have to give your life for faith, then be ready to die for Christ. You will receive your blessing in the kingdom of God; there you will live forever and receive the crown of life."

My father had a different manner of speaking with me. Like a teacher or a legislator, he would break things down for me to make his point clear, as if he was signing an executive order that wasn't subject to change.

Once when I was getting ready to go out into the streets with my friends, I heard how my mother prayed in her room, "God, bless Ivan for ministry, reveal to him his calling and bless his life." I was listening to her while holding onto the front door handle. In that moment there was a battle inside me to go or to stay home. I stood there in thought until she finished praying. After a few seconds, I returned to my bedroom and lay down to sleep.

The prayers of my mother and father influenced me more than my own desires. My Bible school was the time spent in my parent's house. Although we didn't study the theory, the practice was more than enough.

When I was a teenager, I was arrested for preaching the gospel. Three times my parents were fined thirty rubles because of me, and of course, my mother always came to the court with me.

The authorities would have forgiven me for various mischief without forcing me to pay fines if I was a member of Komsomol, but I was not, and I was guilty of nothing but faith. My mother told me the following during our trips to the court, "Look, Son, here is the difference between you and them, they can act against the law, but you cannot. Live righteously, hope in the Lord, and He will take care of you."

She consoled me all the time and asked me not to worry, emphasizing happily that I was different. I grew up not with the consciousness of guilt, but with happiness.

If I could choose who I'd like to be, I would definitely like to have my father's anointing and my mother's character. A couple of years ago, I was present in Ukraine at her eightieth birthday. I didn't notice any specific changes in her. She was as cheerful as before. I wish I was able to show her all the grandchildren and great-grandchildren, who are more than forty in number. We have not gathered with the whole family for twenty-nine years. My mother is still the same; she blesses us every day, encourages me so that my heart belongs only to Jesus, and whatever happens in my life and ministry, to remain faithful to God. "Even if you didn't get what you wanted or dreamed of, stay faithful to Jesus," she says.

Mom still continues to pray and believes for all of her family to stay close to God and serve Him. I became the person that my father and mother wanted me to be. This is not my merit at all. Now, as a father, I raise my children to look like my wife and me. I try to do everything in my power to help them grow as faithful people in the Lord.

Does a mother play an important role in the family? Yes, she does. A mother reflects the character, love, and the qualities of how an individual should be, which, along with her care, she passes on to her child. Mother's words have a greater influence than school, peers, TV, and the Internet. Everything a mother says to her child is like a prophecy that not a single Bible school is able to give. Children grow up preserving the words of their mothers in their hearts, which at the due time grows and bears fruit. If the tree has weak roots, how can it become a strong tree? It will neither bear fruit nor have healthy growth. The words of a mother not only strongly influence the child; but repentance is another strong foundation for a person's life. I am glad that I was growing both spiritually and physically because my mother set an example of a commited Christian in everything she did. I can say that my personal spiritual birth took place alongside my birth. Everything happened the way it did because my mother respected God and her husband and loved all of us. My mother is my role model of how a mature believer should be.

NADEZHDA KLIMENKO

The youngest daughter talks about her mother

Whenever I get into trouble, I always think about how my mother would act in this situation. My mother is amazing. While growing up, I never heard her murmur or complain; whatever she did, she was always happy with it. My mother gave birth to eighteen children, and only sixteen of them stayed alive. There are more than sixty grandchildren, and great-grandchildren are just popping up, and according to our recent calculations, there are 120 people in our family in total. I think soon this number will be doubled.

I live far away from my mother now. I serve in Russia, and my mother and father live in Seattle, USA. My parents were born in Ukraine but moved to Russia after their marriage. Many years later, another move was waiting for our family. We moved to America, where our relatives live to this day. Not all of them, though. Like me, some of my relatives settled in Russia.

Honestly, I have never seen my mother sad and or complaining, and she has never initiated conflicts in our house. I'm not exaggerating. She never raised her voice to us; she was always cheerful and happy. I think my mother's distinctive characteristic was the genuine love that she had toward people.

We have a large family, not because it had to be that way or because my parents followed religious traditions. My mother dreamed of having twenty children. Although she hasn't fulfilled her plan, our large family was an opportunity for great gossip.

All our relatives, neighbors, and non-believers who knew our family grumbled that the children were growing up in poverty. They genuinely wondered why our parents needed such a large horde of hungry mouths.

But we never lived in poverty. Even though my father was not very literate, he worked hard and earned good money. When we were little, we saw how my father brought home a wad of money and put it on the shelf. He bought all the best things for us, and we had everything that we needed in our house. Even when we lived in the village, my father had the best motorcycle among the neighbors; oh, yes, he loved to ride it.

Years ago, my mother and father had to wake up at five o'clock in the morning, because there was a lot of work to be done around the house before going to work. But now that the children have grown up, my father sleeps until seven. "God gives his beloved a rest," he says with a smile. My mother, on the contrary, started sleeping worse with age. Sometimes she suffers from insomnia; that's why she gets up earlier than everyone else in the house.

Whenever I complain of fatigue and malaise, I remember that my mother never said that she was running out of strength. She underwent knee replacement surgery recently. After that, she managed to visit two states and be part of her grandson's wedding, despite the fact that she is a little over eighty years old.

While growing up, our acquaintances often said that my mother was probably cooking borsh in huge cooking pots for a week in advance just to feed us all. However, I always woke up from the smell of my mother's tasty dishes. She made us crepes, fried potatoes, and the best pierogis in the world.

In Russia, our school was not far from our house, and quite often my classmates came home with me. My mother fed everyone and talked with us. My classmates loved to come to our house. Since then, nothing has changed. Her children and grandchildren love her dearly. She is our beam of light that attracts all the relatives to her. We run home with great joy just to be next to her.

If you only knew how much I love my mother's poppy seed pies and her delicious crepes with curds. Now she feeds her grandchildren, saying, "It's accepted to say in your country,

SISTERS

'What is given as a present, cannot be given away,' but here we say, 'Whoever comes here eats soup.'" With these words, she pours the soup into a bowl and watches with care while we eat.

I don't remember my childhood well, but what has remained in my memory is my mother's endurance. She was so strong that she went through both pregnancy and childbirth calmly. It's not an easy job to take care of a large family, but she managed to do it—and with a smile.

After her fourth pregnancy, my mother had a dream in which an old woman told her the following words, "You won't live long after conceiving your fifth child. You will give birth to your child, but no one will be next to you. Death awaits you."

Soon my mother was pregnant with her fifth child, my brother Anatoli, and she didn't give in to fear. She didn't pay attention to that dream. The time came for my mother to deliver her baby, and my father had just returned from a business trip. The delivery process had already begun when my father went to the neighboring village for a doctor. Without waiting for the doctor, my mother delivered the baby alone. She lost a lot of blood, but she handled it.

You may wonder how she did it. I believe it is because she had a solid faith in God, and that He was next to her, and gave her strength to go through that trial. Her trust in the Lord was accompanied by such peace and warmth that it was enough for the whole family.

After giving birth to another child, my mother was usually kicked out of the maternity hospital with the following words, "We will not accept you anymore."

She didn't listen to them, and every year and-a-half, she went to the hospital to give birth to another boy or girl. My mother never thought about herself. She gave life to her children and took care of them until they grew up and created their own families.

Speaking of daughters, I remember my mother's numerous daughters-in-law. She loves them all as her own daughters. I think it's because she didn't have the same kind of relationship with her mother-in-law. For a long time, my mother and father lived with my father's parents, and despite a very offensive attitude from the adults' side, my mother always said the following, "I'm going to love my daughters-in-law like my own daughters and maybe even more." Consequently, that's the way it was. Even the girls who are not related to our mother by blood love and take care of her because their affection is mutual and genuine.

My mother would say, "I don't understand those women who have two or three children and say that they are so naughty they can't cope with them. My sixteen children were so great that I had no problem bringing them up."

I believe my mother said it sincerely. She trusted the Lord so much that she never thought about anything bad. She was not afraid for us, but she brought us up to the Creator of heaven in prayers every day. She believed that everything would be okay in her childrens' lives. She didn't allow herself to doubt that God would abandon her family or that one of her children would fall into bad influence.

During my school years, I noticed more than once how God protected me from committing bad deeds. My friends were free to do whatever they wanted to; but it felt like I was behind an invisible line and that was why I was able to keep myself clean. I saw how the youngsters smoked. Whenever they went to a club or a disco, although I wanted to speak to them, I waited them outside and never shared their love for such type of entertainments. So my mother's faith and prayer kept me from unnecessary pain.

My mother and father never forced us to pray with them, but I heard them pray every morning, and we fell asleep to the sound of their songs and communication with the Lord every evening. They began and ended their day with God, and I knew for sure they spent most of their time on their knees.

Everything comes from the family, doesn't it? My parents lived the way they taught us to live. Actions really do speak louder than words.

Whenever I look into my father's eyes, I see sincerity and holiness. I am quite sure he is not afraid to die. My father is a man of faith. They had many difficulties in life, but I never came to know them as a child. My mother and father spared us from all the problems, solving them on their own. That's why I can clearly state that I lived in a sort of a vacuum, happy and careless. I encountered real life problems when I was a grown-up living in America. Whenever I encountered problems, I chose to follow my parents' path because I had witnessed the fruit of their patience.

My parents went to church every Sunday, and the only reason they would ever miss a church meeting was when they were in the hospital. This tradition has passed from my parents to us, and from us to our children, and a mandatory visit to church is rooted in the value system of our family. It's a great joy and blessing for us. Although they didn't accept a refusal when it concerned going to church, they gave us freedom to act according to our own conscience in other things. They never told us, "You have to pray like this, or you have to do things this or that way."

What I actually witnessed was how my father and mother served with a great joy and loved helping others, and I wanted to do the same. Almost every evening was spent with my family at prayer meetings. Later, I began actively serving in church in addition to my household duties. I happily used all my free time serving at church.

My mother loved to work. I can't say she did it because we needed something; she simply loved working in addition to her household duties. That's why we all grew up to be active people in life. Children worked with the adults in the vegetable garden on equal basis when we lived in Bataysk. Some of us even laughed, telling mom, "When we grow up, we will roll the garden up in asphalt."

My mother had an amazing ability to work tirelessly, and instead of ten seedlings she could take care of twenty, in which case we needed to help her. Despite the large family and many responsibilities, we managed to do everything. And my mother encouraged and motivated us by creating little occasions for joy.

The eldest children and my father divided the chores around the house between themselves, and the young ones learned while helping the others. I spent a lot of time in the kitchen helping my mother to cook borsh, since the first grade.

You might wonder if the behavior of the ministers ever caused a sense of resentment in the family? No, I don't remember anything like that, but once my brother wasn't allowed to get baptized. The whole family prepared for this day, so we weren't happy, but I think my parents just told the ministers their thoughts about the matter, but getting offended or resentful was out of the question.

The relationship between my father and mother was very warm, without unnecessary tenderness. We didn't hear our parents use such words as "you are beautiful" or "you are cute." My mother never raised her voice to my father; I remember that very well. She always spoke with him gently and with respect. I don't remember even one case when me and my brothers witnessed their disputes.

I addressed my parents very respectfully. Perhaps this is a Ukrainian tradition, but I look at it as an expression of respect for elders. My brothers fell silent when dad spoke up as he entered the room. We listened carefully to our parents when they spoke with us. This is how we were brought up.

One day my brother Valentine said the following while all of us were gathered around the table, "Mom, you made one mistake in your life."

"Tell me, tell me what I have done," my mother smiled.

"You gave birth to way too many executives," he said, and they both smiled.

During the times when most of the children had to attend university, it was very difficult for the children of believers to get a graduate degree. My older brothers took part in various scholastic competitions and won first place awards. However, they couldn't get graduate degrees. In spite of this, we all grew up to be hard working and successful, each in his own sphere.

After moving to Russia, my older brothers bought cars for themselves when they were eighteen because, just like my father, they worked hard and wholeheartedly. One of my brothers is the head of a construction company in Bataysk, another one is engaged in an oil-refining business, and the third one manages security firms in the Rostov region. Now each of them has his own business. So you see that having many children is not a problem; it's a blessing!

My mother loves to be around young people and give them candy. She even sends parcels to Ukraine. We calculated that she had sent over one hundred boxes in one year. That's her heart; so big that it reaches not only to her own relatives, but to the other people who surround her.

My mother sometimes says, "If we help someone today, someone else will give a helping hand to our children tomorrow."

Recently, my mother went to church to have some fellowship with her friends after the service. They are considerably younger than her. One of them is over fifty and the other ones are older than her. While they were there, each of them started telling my mother about all their physical challenges. My mother was surprised, "I am over eighty, but I feel so good! I'd rather have a fellowship with young people."

Many funny stories happened to my mother. I remember once that she told me a story of how someone tried to rob her on the bus. "I was sitting on the bus, and suddenly it felt like someone was reaching into my pocket. My wallet was in that pocket, but it was completely empty. I should have left some pocket change there."

There was a time when my mother lost her hearing, but she accepted it with joy. "It's good that I won't be able to hear anything temporarily," she said. "Because a raven flies to my window every morning and wakes me up, so now I can sleep peacefully."

My mother looks at life optimistically and invariably with faith. She is like a guiding star on our way to God. That light inside of her is where she carries her calling of a mother, wife, and Christian.

MARIA SAMOYLICH

Have I ever talked with my children about God? Of course, I have. But I can't tell you how I taught them that. I remember that we prayed together, and as for faith and respect for God, they acquired it themselves as a gift from above, not as something imposed by me or my husband. Not all the children knew God when they learned to speak. My son Slava experienced an amazing presence of the Holy Spirit when he was sixteen years old. He said that until that moment he didn't have such an "appetite" neither for the Word of God or for the presence of the Lord, but at that moment, Slava realized that God was real and began to pray.

All of our children experienced nearly the same thing in their lives. I think that this made their faith stronger. They were brought up in God's presence and chose to continue to live their lives together with God.

SISTERS

We did not idealize people at church, but we also didn't allow our children think badly of someone. We also didn't raise our voice to someone at all in our house. My children didn't know what a dispute was unless it was their childish fights.

Sometimes people would ask if my children or family was influenced by bad preachers or ministers. I don't know of any that we encountered, and that was why I didn't find it necessary to discuss somebody's conduct or ministry. It's better to worship the Lord and pray for needs than blame people for their blunders.

My children grew up with an ideal picture of the world, but not because we sheltered them from the world. It's not like that at all. Many people came to church meetings from different cities and settlements, and when they were talking to one another after the meeting, it turned out that these people were looking for a place to spend the night or to stay for couple of days until they returned home. They either rented a room or stayed in Christians' houses. Our family usually hosted those who had no place to go and had no means to pay for rent.

During those days, my husband, Samuel, and I served the guests all the tasty things that we had stored in our cellar. We would set a big table. Sometimes the children stayed hungry because the food simply disappeared from the table within seconds.

I used to cook a lot and often. We served the food from a big serving dish so everyone was able to take as much food as they wanted. Not all the children ended up getting as much food as they wanted, so we would say, "You snooze, you lose." It became a common saying in our house!

Our house was not very big. It was only a kitchen and the living room. Although we slept like sardines packed in a can, there was enough room for everyone. Sometimes we could fit five people in one bed. Of course, this only happened when we had guests with us.

Samuel and I became parents to ten amazing children who grew up to become ministers and pastors of various churches. But if you came to our house many years ago and saw how noisy and crowded it used to be when we were having guests, you would doubt that our children had enough parental care. It was quite normal for us to sacrifice our own benefits for the sake of serving others. Maybe we didn't pay much attention to our children, but they had enough love.

Modern authors of books on parenting may condemn us for taking care of our children in a completely different way than what's written in those books. However, I tried to do my best to bring them up as people genuinely loving God.

My son reminded me of a story that may seem a bit trivial to you, but I like it's meaning.

Once Samuel was ploughing the field. In order to cultivate the soil, the whole family would come together and use our hands to take care of every centimeter of the land. We didn't have our own tractor or any special equipment.

149

SISTERS

One day, a tractor drove around the collective farm, and an employee could quickly plough our plot of land for 100 grams of vodka. But my husband didn't give a drink to the tractor driver, believing that he would renounce his own principles by yielding to him. That day we worked till late night. Not all the children understood their father's intentions, however, I know they were proud of him.

Samuel and I supported each other in our decisions, even when it concerned disciplining the children. Our children didn't even think to complain about me or their father. They knew quite well that they could get worse punishment. I never complained about my husband either; I did my best to understand him and be grateful for everything he did for us.

No matter how much money my husband earned and no matter how hard it was at times, the Lord always helped our family to live in joy.

I don't consider myself to be a saint because I prayed less or because I allowed my children to listen to the radio and read books. My husband and I also kept up with the news; the newspaper was a big part of our daily lives.

An atmosphere of respect and obedience was the most important thing in the relationship between me and the children. At the same time, they did not need to be afraid or ashamed of us. I did not set a high benchmark for my children, I tried to love them the way the Lord loved us. For me, it meant accepting my family with all its shortcomings.

***

Slava Samoylovich, the youngest son

In our village, we had neither dancing clubs or other types of clubs. The church ministers were able to create such respectable atmosphere at church, and it made us feel good together. There was no urge to look for entertainment anywhere else. A young generation grew up without bad influences.

Until my personal encounter with God, I tried to respect and obey my parents. In return, they trusted me and allowed me to go to the library and pick up the books that interested me the most. Of course, I don't consider myself a saint, but the reson I know God today is because of my family and the church. .

***

The children did not always work or graze the cows in the fields with joy. They complained to their father, talking about other families as example. "Dad, the others have one cow and we have two. They graze their cows for one day and we graze them for two days. And we have twice as much land as others! Dad do you understand?" the children wanted their father to take pity on them.

But he simply answered them, "Children, we have no time for reasoning. Cram it in and break it out. Less words, more action."

So that was how we lived without hesitation and complaints. I agree, we worked hard; but while working, the days were flying by so quickly that I remember them with joy. I remember how we sang our favorite songs with my husband. The two of us glorified the Lord, singing one hymn after the other:

"I love Your house, Oh Lord.
The place where Your love prevails.
And I love the church,
Full of people redeemed by Christ. "

Do you know what joy fills your heart when you come home tired and see your family? You sit down at the table together, have a quick dinner, and then go to finish your household chores singing love songs to Christ. At that point, there's no place left for envy or regret for having a better life. We were glad for what we had!

We wanted our children to live in the present—not in fantasies or dreams. Simultaneously, faith was the main anchor.

Samuel and I trusted the Lord in everything. If we had nothing to eat today, then God would help us get food tomorrow. Miracles happened when we prayed to God on our knees. God answered our prayers more than once.

I can't explain you with words how much love and respect I have toward God in my heart. But I hope that my life perfectly reflects what I feel inside.

But Samuel wasn't always a Christian. My husband came to know the Lord in a very interesting way. One day when he was twenty-two years old, he was laying next to a fence, drunk and forgotten by his friends. One of the parishioners of our church was passing by. Noticing a dying man on the ground, he lifted him up and took him to the church meeting. When Samuel found himself at church, he instantly came to his senses and sobered up. He repented, and from that day on, he never drank again. After a while, he was put in prison for his faith.

Stalin was in power those days. At the court, my husband was sentenced to twenty years of imprisonment, nine out of which he had to spend in Kyrgyzstan, in a place named Osh. In the following years, he couldn't come closer than one thousand kilometers to his birthplace.

Samuel had already served three months of his sentence in Osh when we received the news that Stalin was dead. My husband miraculously fell under an amnest. He was given a soldier's watch-coat and was kicked out of the prison. He had neither money nor documents, but he returned home.

The story of how I met my husband is very simple. We met at church, and after a while we realized that we could not live without each other so we arranged a wedding.

Honestly, my husband's relatives did not accept our decision; my faith was strange to them. I am from a Baptist church, and Samuel and all his relatives are Orthodox. Despite this, my husband and I lived in harmony.

We witnessed various miracles in our life. It will take a lot of time to tell them all, but I'd like to share two stories that happened to me.

SISTERS

When I was pregnant with my last son, I don't remember exactly if I was in the fifth or sixth month of pregnancy, suddenly the baby started dropping, and I realized that I was losing him. It happened in the vegetable garden, where I was digging the vegetable patches. I suddenly felt as though I was about to deliver the baby earlier than the delivery date , so I fell on my knees and prayed to God, asking, "Lord, You gave life to nine of my children. Please, don't forsake this tenth one."

I set there for a while, and after a few minutes my belly started to move back to where it was supposed to be. Everything calmed down inside me. At the appointed time, I gave birth to Slava, our last child.

Our youngest son is our miracle. God protected him not only when he was in my womb, but after his birth too. Slava was barely five years old when a motorcycle fell on him. He was playing next to the motorcycle when it suddenly fell on him. My son died in front of my eyes, but I was praying for his resurrection. The ambulance was late, and Slava was in my arms, and he was not breathing. When Samuel heard me scream, he jumped straight down from the attic. I don't even know how he didn't break anything, but God protected him too. He ran to us and also began to pray to the Lord for help. Our friends from the church gathered around us, and we all cried out to God.

Someone was pouring out water on Slava. Something was happening around us, but I kept praying until our son was resurrected. I will not forget that moment. Suddenly my boy was alive, and we were praising God, hardly understanding what just happened in front of our eyes.

I received a medal from Brezhnev for my youngest son that has a commemorative inscription "Mother-heroine," but my best reward was always knowing that my children grow up in a fellowship with the Lord. And oh, how quickly they all grew up!

The hardest thing for me was being separated from my children. While leaving for the army, my eldest sons often sent me letters and photographs. I wasn't worried about the fact that there would be more work to be done around the house, but rather it was the absence of my beloved children that weighed down on me.

I remember one day when my youngest son came up to me while I was cooking. Seeing my tears, he said, "Mom, when I leave for the army, I will not send you letters or photographs."

I asked him wiping away my tears, "Why is that, son?"

"So that you won't cry anymore," he said triumphantly.

It doesn't matter where my children are going or for how long they are going to stay there, I always pray for them. And God kept them all, for which I am grateful to this day.

***

Slava Samoylovich, Maria's son

As a child, we love our mothers; as we grow up, we respect them. The love mothers have for their children is sincere, and they never complain if things go wrong or when parenting is difficult or painful. Only God knows what our mothers went through while they raised us.

TAMARA ARBUZOVA

My name is Tamara Arbuzova, and I will tell you a little bit about my family and children. I gave birth to fourteen children and I have around sixty grandchildren. I remember all my children's, grandchildren's, and great-grandchildren's names, but I don't remember when their birthdays are.

I was born into a family where they did not speak openly about God. My father and mother didn't go to church. It's true that you could go to prison as a criminal for your faith during those years. And the churches were open only in Moscow.

My mother used to read the gospel for me, and that was how I became a believer. My father was an atheist, and it was very difficult to communicate with him. He returned from the war as a very reserved person. He only spoke occasionally about what he had to endure at the battlefield, and I started to fear him. Nobody ever explained me that people who saw such terrible things had gone through a trauma, and that you need to approach them differently. I avoided getting in contact with my father because I was little and didn't understand a lot of things, although he never laid a finger on me.

When I grew up, I learned a little bit about the war from my relatives. So when my mother was seeing my dad off to war, she hid a religious symbol in his soldier's shirt. God has saved my dad many times. Dad told how the enemies surrounded them and how he was the only who stayed alive out of his whole detachment. Barely understanding what was happening, he managed to reach to another detachment. But even there, almost everyone was killed. My dad was instructed to get into a car with wounded soldiers, so he jumped into the nearest car to get out of the occupied territories.

I think you would like the story of how my parents met. In my mother's documents, it was written kulak's daughter.[1] She wasn't able to get a job and it was hard for her to live. My dad came into the picture when my mother had just turned sixteen. My dad originally was from Belarus, but I have no idea how he got to the Far East. He approached to my mother's parents with a proposal of marriage. They did not refuse him, but did not give permission for the wedding either. "What do you want

---

1. A wealthy or prosperous peasant who usually owned a large farm and could hire workers and lease land.

from us? You know very well who we are and that our daughter is a daughter of kulak, it's not easy to live with such a person."

It wasn't just about my mother, but also the fact that my father was twenty-seven and she was only sixteen years old at that time. Eleven years of age difference is not a joke! But seeing my father's serious intentions, my grandparents gave in and allowed him to marry their daughter. After the wedding, dad took my mother and left the city. So this is their love story.

My parents had four children—two sons and two daughters. We lived well and worked hard.

I remember when I was a young girl and my uncle Vladimir Govor lived with us in our house. He was the first one who gathered the Christians from all over the area in our house. Believers hid in their homes; no one wanted to speak about God, but my uncle invited people over to our house and even for prayer. He was looking for a wife, but he couldn't find anyone among the Christian girls. So he went over to the Baptists. He really didn't want to marry a Baptist, but what he could do? There was a girl Vladimir took a liking to, and he got engaged with her. We had a physharmonica, a type of primitaive piano or reed organ, at home, someone played the instrument, and everyone else sang. We glorified God. This is how the first group of Christians appeared in our area. We began to get together and pray, and then the Lord baptized me and my uncle's bride with the Holy Spirit. After that they got married.

SISTERS

My husband was born in Svobodny, and I lived in Belogorsk. It was two hours' drive from his house to mine. He often visited us together with his friends. After a couple of visits, we got married.

We could have never imagined with Volodya that we would have fourteen children. Yes, it's only accepted among Christians that despite the fact how many children God gives you, you will be able to set them on their feet. Maybe that's hard, but that was how they were preaching to us, and since then, nothing has changed.

14 Children
54 Grandchildren
19 Greatgrandchildren

I remember that at times my pregnancies were so hard that I didn't want to have babies anymore, but my conscious didn't allow me to kill a child. I gave birth to all of my children.

We had to work hard to feed our family. We had our own house and a huge household to take care of. We kept a cow, pigs, and took care of our vegetable garden. In the greenhouse we grew cucumbers, and had different types of vegies growing on the ground, which we sold in the market. We were not able to buy a car because we couldn't afford it, but we managed to do everything quite well. We didn't live in poverty and we had enough food and everything.

My husband is an A-grade electrician. He was working, and we were taking care of the household. In the evenings I worked as a cleaner. When I wasn't working, I was busy around the house. On top of it all, I was sewing clothes for the children and for me and my husband. Honestly, I would make a good dressmaker.

Oh, how many swaddling clothes I washed while the children were little! I didn't own a washing machine until I already had four kids. And then I had to wait for a year until I was able to buy it. It was pretty nice and round shaped. Before getting the washing machine, I washed both linen and the swaddling clothes by hand.

How did we cook? We cooked either in buckets or cooking pots. Sometimes I would cook up a bucket of cabbage rolls or okroshka in the mornings, and when I returned home in the evening, all I found was an empty bucket. I started cooking again the next morning. This is how we lived.

We loved going to see our friends and relatives, and loved having guests too. When were together, we either prayed or glorified God. What good and joyful times those were! I don't know why, but the guests loved to gather at our house. I still remember how we celebrated the holidays; our house was always noisy and crowded. Everyone was eating and glorifying God.

No one left our house hungry. When our guests were getting ready to leave, I would give each one of them a jar of milk or jam. So it was a tradition in our family.

The sound of prayer was always heard from our house. My husband once told me how he stood under the windows and listened to me pray in Spirit. I loved praying. I prayed to God for my children, for our neighbors, and for any needs I was aware of. Things have changed now. Sometimes I feel so bad that that even my prayers are different. Yes, the past years were very different from now. Sometimes when I realized that one of my children departed from God or an illness was holding them captive, I knelt down and prayed to God, and I didn't stop praying until everything was settled.

My children encountered difficulties at school; they suffered for their faith. But what could we do? After graduating from school, they wanted us to send our children to universities, but I rejected the offer saying, "You don't have to make communists out of my children; you will not let them finish their studies anyway, and will ask something in return from us."

My husband was often invited to the KGB for an interrogation. They even preformed a house search, looking for religious literature, and then they imprisoned him for fifteen days.

Here is how it happened. In 1980, the Summer Olympics were being held in Moscow, and the local authorities were worried that Volodya would leak information to foreign sources. Therefore, they took him to prison, and afterward, decided to put him in jail for a long period of time. Both my husband and the presbyter were judged and sentenced to seven years of prison. Although Volodya actively participated in church life, he succeeded in averting the same fate.

Everything turned out how God planned. My daughter worked as a nurse, and she found a note from her father, which read, "They have already taken my fingerprints and want to imprison me."

I didn't hesitate to write a letter to Brezhnev, saying that my husband had been imprisoned, and I would not be able to feed thirteen children alone, so I asked him to set Volodya free. Together with our pastor, we delivered the letter, and later we received an answer saying, "Set him free." My husband had to sign an acknowledgement of travel restrictions. Volodya returned home, where his friends were waiting for him. They drove my husband to an aerodrome in Essentuki and from there he flew to Nakhodka.

The next day, some people came to our house, and all of them were asking the same question, "Where is Vladimir Tikhonovich? Where is he?" I remember answering them, "He is not here. Don't look for him anymore because he is not coming back."

Volodya and our eldest son bought a house in Nakhodka, and sent us a telegram to come over there. We sold all of our property in Krasnodar. It was a pity to leave that amazing and rich region. There were always plenty of apples and whatever your heart desired. But there weren't any jobs.

So that's how we ended up in the North, and later on in America. Thirty years have passed since I left the Soviet Union.

Volodya died when most of our children were grown up and some of them were even married. At that point, nine of my children still lived with me, so I had to continue to some- how feed and shoe everyone. We began to sow potatoes in the fields in large quantities. Some of my children did the work about the house, and the rest took care of the vegetable garden. I can say that labor saved us. Frankly speaking, I had to send some of my children to my married sister's house to ease my burden.

What more can I say about this life? Everything is temporary. Heaven is what we all are aiming for. I came to this understanding throughout my life, and I am very happy for that. Life here on earth flies by so fast. I am telling you all this, yet at the same time, it seems as if all of this happened yesterday.

I don't consider myself a hero; I'm an ordinary woman. Although I trusted the Lord, I didn't stop working for a second. Now my grandchildren are taking care of me. There was a season when I was bedridden for three weeks because of toxemia, and during that whole period of time, my relatives did not leave me. One of my grandchildren even took me to church to take Holy Communion. I am very grateful to him for that.

Life was not easy, but a person gets a reward for everything. Wherever I look, I have either a son, a daughter, or grandchildren. Everyone takes care of me, and they look forward to my visits. I am not a scandalous person, that's why my relatives love having me as a guest. I find it much easier to admonish either my son or my daughter than my son-in-law or my daughter-in-law.

SISTERS

What I find interesting is that now people have dogs instead of children. Nowhere in the Bible you will find such a command, that people should have more dogs than children. Maybe I didn't go to the resorts or was deprived of some entertainment, but I was happy, and no one in my family went hungry.

If a mother wants to get to know her children, she needs to take care of them. What did God say in His Word? "Be fruitful and multiply." This is how my husband and I lived. I had friends who are no longer alive, and they had no children and died as old maids. I wonder who remembers them now?

Scan the code below with your phone to access Pastor Artur's social media channels.

Made in United States
Orlando, FL
14 January 2022

13425569R00095